PEACE
BE
WITH
YOU

John 20:19

PEACE
BE
WITH
YOU

Cornelia Lehn

Faith and Life Press
Newton, Kansas

Faith and Life Press

Library of Congress Number 80-70190
International Standard Book Number 0-87303-061-3
Printed in the United States of America
Copyright © 1980 by Faith and Life Press
718B Main Street, Newton, Kansas 67114

Illustrated by Keith R. Neely
Design by John Hiebert
Printing by Mennonite Press, Inc.

Dedicated to the memory of my father

Foreword

History has been generous in providing a legacy of war stories. Children have admired the bravery of warriors from the biblical David who conquered the Philistines, to France's Napoleon whose appetite to conquer was never fully satisfied. There is no scarcity of war heroes!

But what of peace heroes? *Peace Be With You* is evidence that there is also a strong legacy of peace stories. Cornelia Lehn has uncovered the stories of many peace heroes whose courage, convictions, and peace tactics surpass that of the combatant soldier; however, many of these stories have never been published. Carefully researched from historical materials and from oral tradition, the stories are living and colorful testimony that many people throughout the centuries believed and lived the Christian way of peace, even when confronted by the most violent of circumstances.

This peace story project was initiated by the General Conference and Mennonite Church peace and social concerns offices. We discussed the project with our respective committees and the staff of the Mennonite Central Committee Peace Section. All agreed that a collection of stories about peace suitable for children would be an excellent peace education resource. We noted that for adults there are growing numbers of books and study materials providing a biblical, theological, and practical basis for peacemaking. But with a few notable exceptions (*Coals of Fire, Twelve Becoming, Henry's Red Sea*), resources suitable for peace education with children are few.

Thus, two major factors prompted us to commission the writing of *Peace Be With You.* First is the continuing need for peace education materials for children. Children learn by observ-

ing *living* examples of peacemakers. They also learn by *hearing* stories of people who lived the way of peace.

A second factor is that there are many peace stories coming out of our biblical and Mennonite heritage that have gone "begging" for a writer. There *are* peace heroes. Many of these stories of unsung heroes modeling peace and reconciliation were in the memories of people living today or on forgotten pages of history. These most powerful peace testimonies needed to be captured while those who know the stories best are still here to tell us.

Peace Be With You is a resource for parents and teachers to help them share the Christian way of peace with children and youth. The stories are written so they can be read to children or be told with adaptations for particular age-groups and for special needs. Young people and children can also read the book for themselves and will find it a very readable source of inspiration and growth.

We gratefully acknowledge the Schowalter Foundation for helping make this book possible through a special grant. We owe much to Cornelia for her skill and dedication to the unending hours of research and writing that went into the preparation of this manuscript. And we acknowledge with love and appreciation the lives of the many people in the stories within these pages who discovered the joy of living the Christian way of peace. We challenge readers of this book to follow the legacy of Christian peacemaking.

Harold R. Regier
Hubert Schwartzentruber

Preface

Often, when I was a child, my father and I sat on an old rocker in front of the fire. As we watched the moon come up over the Saskatchewan prairie, we talked about many things. But sooner, or later, I would say, "Now tell me about the time when you were a little boy."

And so my father told me about life as he had known it. But he told me much more. He told me about the lives of those who had gone before us—people who had dared to live and die for their faith, people all through the centuries who had taken Christ seriously.

I realize now that my father passed on to me priceless treasures of our faith in the form of stories. It seems natural to me, therefore, that in wanting to pass on these treasures to the next generation, I should also do it in the form of stories.

The stories in this book come from many countries and cover a time span from the first century to the present. I had a fascinating time finding the stories. Some I was aware of through previous reading, some I came upon by browsing around in libraries, and some came to me in most unexpected ways through other people. The source for each story is given on the acknowledgment page in the back of the book.

Most of the incidents around which the stories are woven are historical, some are legendary, but all of them, I trust, are contemporary in their development and implication.

I would like to thank my many friends who helped me in my search, and who pointed me to people who had stories to tell. A special thank-you to the Mennonite Library and Archives at Bethel College for making available to me the tapes of its Oral History Project.

Alvin Beachy, Herta Funk, John Gaeddert, Robert Kreider, Don Kaufman, Harold and Rosella Regier, and Blanche Spaulding read the manuscript critically and made many helpful suggestions. I am deeply grateful.

It is my hope that pastors, teachers, and other adults will find this book helpful when they are looking for stories to tell. I wrote the stories with older juniors, young people, and intergenerational groups in mind. Above all, however, I hope that families will like to read the book aloud, a story at a time, during quiet times at home or in a camp setting.

The stories my father told me helped to shape my faith. May the Holy Spirit also use the stories in this book to direct the lives of young people as they seek to follow Christ in the nuclear age.

Cornelia Lehn

Table of Contents

PEACE
BE
WITH
YOU

"Peace I leave with you;
my peace I give to you;
not as the world gives do I give to
you.
Let not your hearts be troubled,
neither let them be afraid."

John 14:27 (RSV)

You Shall Have No Other Gods Before Me

Pontius Pilate in Judea A.D. 26-36

Pontius Pilate walked restlessly back and forth in his palace in Caesarea. His brow was wrinkled. "Time to get those Jews to their knees," he muttered angrily.

It was the year A.D. 26, and Pilate had come to Judea as procurator a few months ago. Increasingly the Jews' stubborn resistance to anything that interfered with their religious practices infuriated Pilate. Finally he had enough.

"We shall send the army from Caesarea to Jerusalem to take up their winter quarters there," he said curtly to his commander. "The soldiers are to occupy the city by night and place the standard with the silver image of Emperor Tiberias high on the tower of the fortress of Antonia."

The commander, who had been in Judea for a long time, was stunned. "Your Honor," he said, "the Jewish people will not tolerate it. We have never brought the ensign with the emperor's image into Jerusalem. You see, the Jews believe in one God and will not worship the emperor."

"You have heard my orders," said Pilate. "If the Jews dare to attack the fortress, we will simply put down the revolt and make it clear who has the final authority in this land."

Soon Pilate's army was on its way to Jerusalem.

Silently the soldiers surrounded the city by night.

Carefully they placed the image of the emperor high on the wall of the fortress which overlooked the temple of God.

When the Jews awoke in the morning, they saw, to their horror, the image of Tiberias above the place dedicated to the glory of Jehovah!

The whole city was in an uproar. It was the height of blasphemy. The Word of the Lord said, "You shall have no other gods before me . . . you shall not bow down to them or serve them." And now another god had been placed above the holy temple of God!

But what could they do to remove the image? The city was surrounded by soldiers, fully armed. Any revolt would end in a terrible bloodbath.

No one knows how the decision was made, but on that same day a multitude of Jews began walking to Caesarea. They were going to ask for an interview with Pontius Pilate. Surely they could persuade him somehow to take down the hateful image of the emperor.

When they came to Caesarea they sent a messenger to Pilate to explain their request and to intercede for them.

Pilate came out and stood on his balcony.

As with one voice the Jews shouted, "We beg you, remove the image of the emperor from Jerusalem!"

Pilate merely raised his arm. "Return to Jerusalem," he said coldly. "The image of the emperor will stay where it is. Tiberias is your lord." With that, Pilate went into the house.

He watched the Jews secretly, however. Surely they would go home! What else could they do?

But Pilate was wrong. There was something else they could do. They did not shout. They did not cry. They did not threaten him. To Pilate's utter amazement, he saw the whole mass of people kneel down and pray to their God!

The next morning the Jews were still there. They had brought food along. Apparently they were going to stay. Suddenly Pilate heard them shouting again, "Remove the image of the emperor!"

Pilate ignored the plea, but he became uneasy. All day long the Jews just sat there, talking and murmuring among themselves. It was uncanny

15

to be surrounded by these masses of people. Pilate was certainly not going to take back his word, but how could he get rid of these folks sitting at his doorstep?

For five days the Jews waited in front of Pilate's palace. Every morning at a certain time they shouted the same thing, "Remove the image of the emperor!" Other than that they made no commotion. But Pilate could not forget them. They were there. They got on his nerves.

At last Pilate could stand it no longer. On the sixth day, he ordered the Jews to go to the open place in the city. He would see them there.

Silently and calmly the Jews walked to the center of the city and awaited the arrival of the procurator.

Pilate took his place on the judgment seat. He had asked a whole battalion of armed soldiers to station themselves behind some buildings so the Jews could not see them.

"What is your desire?" Pilate asked the Jews.

"Remove the image of the emperor!" they shouted again.

Pilate had, of course, expected this plea. He gave a signal, and in a moment the soldiers with swords in their hands came out of their hiding and surrounded the Jews.

"Anyone who dares to say one more word about the emperor's image will be killed," shouted Pilate.

A deathly silence hung over the multitude of people.

Then a young Jew walked forward and said to Pilate, "I would rather die than see the emperor's image desecrate the temple of the living God." With that he knelt down and bared his neck to be killed.

In one mighty wave, all the Jews knelt with him. They were ready to die for their faith.

Pilate looked down on the masses. They were on their knees now, but not in subjection to Rome. Should he give the signal for the massacre to begin?

Pilate realized that he had come face to face with something far more powerful than military might! "The image of the emperor will be removed," he said.

The soldiers left, and the Jews arose quietly and walked back to Jerusalem.

Christ Has Sent Me

A story told by Clement of Alexandria about the aged Apostle John

The Apostle John was on a preaching tour in Asia Minor. He liked walking from place to place whenever possible since that gave him time to be alone and to think. Somehow the years had crept up on him. His steps were getting a bit slower and his back was bent. But with the help of a sturdy walking stick, he still managed very well.

After walking up a long hill, he stopped and sat down on a stone by the side of the road. Way down there below him he could see the town he was going to visit. His eyes became bright, and a smile of anticipation crept over his face.

"Philip," he murmured. "I shall see Philip again!"

Philip was very special to the Apostle John. When John had last visited the town several years ago, he had met this youth and had become very attached to him. Philip was quick and friendly, and John was delighted by the intelligent questions he asked. Soon a very warm relationship developed between the Apostle John and young Philip. John felt almost as if he at last had a son. "Good-bye, Father John," Philip had said when they parted. "I will wait every day for your return!"

Now he would see that dear lad again. Since Philip had no parents, John had left him in the care of the bishop of that town. John got up and walked with renewed vigor to his destination.

The bishop welcomed John with open arms and made him comfortable.

"Before we talk about anything else," said John eagerly, "tell me about Philip. Where is he?"

"Oh, John," sighed the bishop, "I knew you would ask about him, but that is a very sad story. As you know, my wife and I took him into our home. We really learned to love him. I taught him myself, and that was pure delight since he was so willing to learn. He decided to become a Christian, and the whole community of believers rejoiced when he was baptized. But then something happened."

"What?" said John impatiently. "Tell me quickly."

"Well, you know how it is," said the bishop sadly. "I was so busy with the work of the church, and after he was baptized I guess I did not spend enough time with him. He got into bad company, and one day they committed a very serious crime. Since Philip was among them, he fled into the mountains with them, and now I hear he has become their chief. It is incredible the acts of bloodshed and cruelty that that band of robbers is committing!"

"And has no one tried to bring Philip back?" cried the Apostle John, jumping up in agitation.

"You don't understand," said the bishop. "They are fully armed. It would be folly to even go near their hideout."

"Well, I am going!" said John. "I am going over there to talk to Philip!"

"No! No! They will kill you," cried the bishop.

But the Apostle John had made up his mind. He made arrangements for a horse and a guide to show him the way to the place in the mountains where they were sure the gang was hiding.

Early the next morning the Apostle John and his guide rode down the trail that John had so recently traveled and then headed into the rocky wilderness.

After several hours on horseback, the guide stopped and said, "Sir, over yonder is the robber's camp. I do not wish to go farther and would advise you to return with me."

"No," said John calmly. "I will go on by myself. You have guided me well, and I thank you for it. Here is the money for your services. Farewell."

The guide galloped away as fast as he could. John continued on his way, gently guiding his horse in the direction of the camp, now clearly visible.

Suddenly two men jumped from behind rocks on either side of the path and grabbed the reigns of John's horse.

"And where do you think you are going, old man?" they yelled roughly, brandishing their swords.

"Greetings, my sons," said the Apostle John. "I would be very grateful to you if you would take me to your captain, Philip. I need to talk to him about an important personal matter."

The two robber guards were somewhat taken aback by this man's serenity and fearless self-assurance. The fact that he was unarmed made them uneasy and unsure of themselves. They took him to Philip's tent.

Just at that moment Philip came out. He stopped short. He couldn't believe his eyes when he saw the Apostle John standing in front of him.

"Father John!" he gasped.

"Yes, my son," said John, holding out his arms, "I have come back at last."

For a moment, Philip stood frozen to the ground. Then the shamefulness of the situation overcame him. He bolted and ran.

But the apostle ran after him. "Philip, Philip," he called, gasping for breath. "Stop! My child, why do you flee from me, your own father, unarmed and aged as I am? Have mercy on me. Don't be afraid. You still have hope. I will explain all this to Christ. If necessary, I will give my life for you, as the Lord died for both of us. Please believe me. Christ has sent me to tell you this."

Philip halted. With his back to John, he looked down. He dropped his dagger. As John came up to him, he turned and threw himself into the apostle's arms and wept.

"Oh, Father John, Father John," he sobbed. "You don't know all the horrible things I have done."

"No, but whatever crime you have committed, Christ, our Savior, has forgiven you!" said John. "Come, let us go home."

John reached for Philip's right hand, but Philip hid it in shame. That hand! It had killed so many people. He could not bear to have the Apostle John touch it.

But John grasped that hand firmly and kissed it. He finally persuaded Philip to come back with him. In the community of believers Philip experienced forgiveness, and with the Apostle John's help he learned what it means to walk in the strength of the Lord.

Finally, the Apostle John could go on his way rejoicing. Philip, his son, had returned to the church!

Second Century

If Your Enemy Is Hungry, Feed Him
The Legend of Servitor

20

Servitor gazed across the Danube River. He was one of the Roman soldiers encamped on the south side of the river for the winter. On the other side he could see the enemy. In the spring, the Emperor Marcus Aurelius, their supreme commander, would himself lead them in the attack. They were to wipe out the barbarian tribes to the north.

But now all was peaceful and strangely quiet, Servitor thought. He had gone to the bank of the river every day, but something different seemed to be going on today. He could not understand it. It looked as if some women and children were venturing much closer to the river than usual. They seemed to be looking for something.

Finally it dawned on Servitor: those people on the other side were hunting for food in the winter. They must be starving!

That night Servitor could not sleep. Before he had left his home on the Tiber River, he had become a Christian. With joy he thought of the other young people with whom he had memorized many passages from the Holy Writings.

Something that Jesus had said now came to his mind: "But I say to you, love your enemies." Those words had always bothered Servitor. He did not know what to make of them. He did not know how to love the enemies his emperor commanded him to kill. Today he had found out something about the enemies on the other side of the river: they were hungry! "If your enemy is hungry, feed him." That is what the great Apostle Paul had written in a letter that was circulating in the Roman churches.

Servitor sat bolt upright on his couch. "Dear God," he whispered, "You can't mean that I am to feed those people on the other side of the river! If I leave the encampment without

permission I will be put to death."

For the rest of the night Servitor tossed restlessly on his bed. He wrestled with two loyalties: his obligation to the Roman emperor and his love for Jesus Christ. He had never thought it would be so hard. But as the sun rose, his mind was made up.

For several days he secretly saved most of the food from his meals and put it in his pouch. Then one morning, when it was still dark, he slipped away from the camp to cross the frozen river.

"Halt! Who goes there?" The voice of the Roman sentry rang out sharp as the crack of a whip.

Servitor started to run, but the sentry was upon him almost immediately.

"Servitor! In the name of common sense, what are you doing?" gasped the sentry when he recognized him.

"Let me go," begged Servitor. "I'm just going to take some food to those poor starving people over there."

"You must be mad," cried the other soldier. "They are our enemies."

"I have been commanded to feed them," said Servitor desperately.

"Well, my fine friend, we shall see about that. I'll take you to the commander of the Guard immediately, and he will decide what to do with you."

The commander, awakened from his sleep, could not believe his ears. "You have orders to feed the enemy!" he said in amazement. "And who, pray, gave such an order?"

"The Lord Jesus Christ," answered Servitor. "He is Lord over all, and I must obey him rather than the emperor."

"Oh, nonsense," grumbled the commander

angrily. "So you are one of those Christians too. Since you have defected to the enemy, I guess I'll have to take you to the emperor immediately."

The Emperor Marcus Aurelius was a thoughtful, philosophical man and dedicated to his duties. He immediately consented to see the commander. "Now, what is the matter?" asked Marcus Aurelius as the commander shoved Servitor into the imperial tent.

"This man was caught deserting to the enemy with food," said the commander. "He says he received an order to feed them!"

The emperor smiled in disbelief. "Well, I certainly never gave you such an order," he said, turning to Servitor.

"I obey my Master, Jesus Christ," said Servitor quietly. "He is Lord of heaven and earth, and he has commanded us to love our enemies. That means feeding them when they are hungry."

"Oh, you Christians," said the emperor wearily. "I know of Christ. It is all so ridiculous.

Feed the enemy, indeed! Starvation is one of our strongest weapons. And those savages out there live like cannibals. Why should we keep them alive?"

"Christ died for all. They, too, need the Savior," said Servitor.

"Enough of that," said the emperor. "The penalty for an act such as yours is death. You know that."

Turning to the commander, the emperor said. "Take this man and let him take his food to the enemy if he wants to. He will find out that death awaits him on the other side of the river also."

The next spring when the Roman army broke up camp and crossed the Danube, a centurion brought the emperor something that he had found. It was a little wooden cross. The emperor turned it around and saw two Latin words scratched on it—"Servitor Christi" (Servant of Christ). Servitor had found his death and his life in the service of his Master.

I Cannot Do Evil
Maximilianus

22 There was great rejoicing in the house of Fabius Victor. They were celebrating the twenty-first birthday of Maximilianus, Fabius Victor's son. And what a fine young man he was! His father was very proud of him. Maximilianus was not only tall and handsome, he also had a great deal of common sense. Fabius was sure he would make a good soldier and be promoted in no time at all. Fabius had already mentioned his name to Dion, the proconsul of Africa.

At the height of the birthday celebrations, Fabius came out with the main surprise.

"Here, Son," he said, "I have had a special coat made for you. You will need it when you enlist in the army." Fabius hung the coat around his son's shoulders.

The guests were so busy exclaiming about the handsome coat that they did not notice how quiet Maximilianus had become. Nobody noticed, that is, except his father. Fabius had looked forward to surprising his son with the coat. He thought he would be very excited about it.

"What is the matter, Son?" asked Fabius. "Don't you like the coat?"

"Oh, yes, yes, of course," replied Maximilianus, drawing his father aside. "What bothers me is that you assume that I will enlist in the army. As you know, I have become a Christian. My Lord bids me love my enemies. How then can I become a soldier? It is impossible!"

Fabius was shocked. "But, Son, I didn't think that your becoming a Christian would make any difference. I knew you always wanted to become a soldier. As a recruiter for the proconsul's army, I have already given Dion your name. You will need to report to him tomorrow."

"If I must report, I must. But I will not become a soldier," replied Maximilianus with his usual determination.

Fabius sighed. Slowly it dawned on him that this situation could become very dangerous. To be a Christian was extremely unpopular. He knew Maximilianus would, with his usual straightforward truthfulness, admit he was a Christian. What would Dion do? Fabius shuddered, and tried to put the thought out of his mind.

The next morning father and son were on their way to see the proconsul, Dion. There had always been a very good relationship between Fabius and his son. How often they had walked together through fields and woods in happier, carefree days!

"Son," said Fabius brokenly, "I am sorry I mentioned your name as a recruit. I would give anything to undo what I did."

"I know, Father," said Maximilianus. "I do not hold it against you. But you understand, don't you, why I cannot become a soldier?"

"Yes," said Fabius. "I understand that if you take Christ's command to love your enemies seriously, you can't do otherwise."

After a strong handclasp, they continued on their way.

Dion consented to see them immediately. "Welcome, welcome!" he cried jovially. "I must congratulate you, Fabius Victor! You have a fine son."

Then, turning to a table nearby, Dion picked up a soldier's badge. "Maximilianus," he said, "here is your badge. Wear it with honor and courage."

Maximilianus did not step forward to receive the badge from Dion's hand. "I am sorry, Sir," he said, "but I cannot serve as a soldier. I am a Christian and must obey Christ as my sovereign

Lord."

The smile faded from Dion's face. "I can't believe my ears," he said. "This is ridiculous. To be a soldier and to serve your country is the most honorable thing you can do. I have heard about these stupid Christians. Surely a fine, intelligent young man like you won't let imaginary religious scruples stand in the way of a brilliant career. Here, take the badge, and I will forget that you are a Christian."

"No," said Maximilianus. "I cannot serve as a soldier. I cannot do evil."

"But I am told there already are Christians in the army and they serve," cried Dion in exasperation.

"They know what is fitting for them," replied Maximilianus, "but I am a Christian and I cannot do evil."

"Evil!" exploded Dion. "Evil! What evil do they do who serve?"

"You know what soldiers do," said Maximilianus, looking straight into Dion's eyes. "They not only kill one man, as a murderer does, but thousands. A crime, multiplied, does not become a virtue."

Dion looked down.

Then he said, "Fabius, you are a recruiter for our army. You know the laws. Persuade your son to change his mind. He must. Otherwise there is only the death penalty."

Fabius became pale. "No," he said. "Even if I could change his mind, I would not. I am proud of my son."

"Then away with you," shouted Dion angrily. At a signal from him, his guards took Maximilianus into custody, and Fabius had to leave the proconsul's chambers.

In agony Fabius walked the streets. "My son, my son," he moaned.

The next morning Maximilianus was executed.

Soon Fabius discovered how deeply the Christian church in Africa was moved by his son's death. As a special honor, the body was brought to Carthage and buried near the tomb of Cyprianus, a great leader in the church, who had also died as a martyr.

The house of Fabius had become silent. But Fabius rejoiced that his son had remained true. "What a son!" he thought. "What a gift to the Lord!"

As the Prophets of Old

Bishop Ambrose   A.D. 390

24   Bishop Ambrose of Milan stood thunderstruck. He had just learned of the murder of seven thousand innocent men in Thessalonica. Someone in that city had murdered the emperor's representative, and in retribution the Emperor Theodosius had ordered all male inhabitants of Thessalonica to be driven into the stadium and hewn down.

Ambrose was shocked and worried. As a servant of God and Bishop of the city of Milan, over which Theodosius was regent, what must he do? Should he reprimand his ruler? The emperor, a Christian, had always been his friend. But the emperor's irresponsible act in Thessalonica showed what he was capable of doing in a fit of anger. Emperor Theodosius might have Ambrose killed for meddling. But to say nothing at all about a sin as terrible as this one was unthinkable.

Ambrose groaned. When he thought of the prophets of old, he knew what he had to do.

On Sunday morning Bishop Ambrose stationed himself just inside the closed doors of the church. The emperor was astounded when he arrived with his retinue. There was no one there to honor him! He struck the doors angrily. Ambrose himself opened them.

"And what does this mean?" demanded Theodosius. "Have you no words of welcome for your emperor when he comes to the doors of your church to take holy communion?"

"Not when he comes with his hands red with the blood of innocent people," said the bishop calmly. "In the name of our Lord, I forbid you to enter this holy sanctuary."

The emperor turned pale with anger. How did the bishop dare to humiliate him in this way in front of his people! A crowd had gathered. They were following this confrontation between their earthly and spiritual rulers with breathless interest.

"I am the ruler of this city!" said the emperor. "No one is going to keep me from walking into this building. Let me pass!"

"The Lord of heaven and earth is over all earthly rulers," said the bishop. "He will not accept you."

"But even King David shed blood," cried Theodosius in exasperation.

"If Your Highness followed King David in sin, then I would suggest that Your Highness also follow him in repentance," said Ambrose.

The emperor turned abruptly and left the church. He knew the bishop was right.

The Emperor Theodosius repented, and after eight months Bishop Ambrose again accepted him into the Church of Christ.

Patrick's Breastplate
St. Patrick

A long, long time ago, a boy called Sucat was captured by pirates and brought from England to Ireland as a slave. During the six years that he was a slave, he became a devoted Christian so that when he finally escaped, he went to France to become a monk. His Latin name was Patricius. In English he was called Patrick or Sucat. As a monk, he prayed long that Christ might show him how he could serve him best.

One night he heard someone calling him. "Sucat! Sucat!"

Patricius, the monk, lifted his head in astonishment. Who could be calling him by his boyhood name?

But he could see no one. He was all alone in his cell in the monastery. He must be dreaming. Patricius turned back to the Holy Writings which he had been studying.

But there was the voice again: "Sucat, Sucat! I am in need of you!"

Now Patricius sensed that there was a bright light in his cell. It must be the Lord!

"Here I am, Lord," said Patricius, trembling all over. "What do you want me to do?"

"I want you to go to Ireland and tell the people there about me. They are ready."

"But—but—Lord," stuttered Patricius before he could help himself, "I escaped from slavery in that country."

"I know," said the voice gently. "Your stay there was your preparation. You are now familiar with the country, the language, and the people. I will be with you wherever you go. I will protect you."

The light faded, but a great joy filled the heart of Patricius. He had his marching orders. Christ had called him tenderly and had used the name his mother had given him. Now Patrick knew

what to do.

As soon as he could, Patrick went to Ireland to proclaim the gospel of Jesus Christ. He was full of enthusiasm and eager to get started, but he still did not quite know how to go about it.

After Patrick landed on the coast of Ireland, he started walking through the country, a knapsack on his back. Wherever he could, he talked and worked with the people. Many of them were friendly and gave him food to take along as he journeyed on.

One day as he was nearing the city of Tara, there was great excitement in the air. Patrick knew that on this night of the year all the people of Ireland worshiped the god of fire in a special service.

The king in Tara had commanded all fires to be extinguished. Then when all the fires were out, the king himself in a solemn ceremony would re-light the fire in his own castle and give homage to the god who, as they believed, gave them the blessing of fire.

Patrick walked along in deep thought. How could he show the king and the people of Ireland that fire was not a god but a gift from the Creator of heaven and earth? How could he make them listen?

Suddenly he had it! In a sheltered place, opposite the castle, he stopped to prepare his supper. He lit his fire and sat down beside it. All around him in the scattered huts and fireplaces, fires were extinguished as the king had ordered. His fire alone burned brightly. Patrick expected something to happen very shortly, and it did.

Several of the king's soldiers came galloping out of the castle grounds and pulled their horses up short in front of Patrick.

"What's the matter with you?" the soldiers

yelled. "Don't you know that the king has decreed that all fires are to be put out? The king is very angry. He saw your fire on the hillside. Come along, fellow. We are to bring you to him!"

The soldiers put out the fire and hurried Patrick into the castle.

The king and the lords and ladies of his court were all assembled in the great hall, ready for the ceremony, when Patrick entered.

They all expected some defiant nobleman. Who else would dare to disobey the powerful king? To their amazement, however, the dignified, stately man who walked into the room carried no sword or spear, nor did he wear expensive clothing. The force of his personality made all the lords and nobles rise to their feet.

The king noticed the involuntary reaction of his court. It angered him.

"Who are you to disobey my command?" cried the ruler of all Ireland. "Do you not know that on this night all fire is to be put out and that I must relight it to honor the god of fire?"

"My name is Patrick," replied the monk. "I have come from a far country to tell you that fire is not a god. There is only one God, the Creator of heaven and earth, who has given us many good gifts. Fire is one of these gifts. When I cooked my supper on the hillside just now, I thanked God for the food and the fire."

The lords and ladies crowded around Patrick. They had never heard of this great and loving God. They wanted to hear more. Patrick took full advantage of this opportunity to tell them of his kind heavenly Father and of his Son, the Lord Jesus Christ.

The king's anger increased. Because his whole court was so taken up with the visitor, however, he decided to wait a bit before taking revenge. In fact, he had to wait quite a while before he could even go on with the ceremony.

The next morning Patrick took his leave. The king did not stop him. Several nobles, however, had seen the look in the king's eyes. "We will show you the way," they said as they accompanied Patrick.

When they had left the king's castle, they said to Patrick, "We can see that the king does not like you. He is still angry. It may be that after some time he will send some of his soldiers after you to kill you. Take this sword and breastplate so that you can defend yourself."

Patrick smiled. "You are very kind," he said, "and I thank you for your thoughtfulness, but I do not need any armor."

The nobles did not quite know what to make of that. Did Patrick wear a secret armor under his cloak, or did he know of some magic that would protect him?

They were worried about his safety nonetheless, so they continued on the way with him for a bit farther.

The dark night was over and the sun was shining brightly. Suddenly a bird began to sing. With that, Patrick, too, began to sing. He was a poet so he made up verses as he went along. He sang:

"I bind unto myself this day
    The power of God to hold and lead,
God's eye to watch, God's might to stay,
    God's ear to harken to my need.
Christ be with me, Christ within me,
    Christ behind me, Christ before me,
Christ beside me, Christ to win me,
    Christ to comfort and restore me."

The nobles listened in amazement to Patrick as he sang.

"That is my breastplate," said Patrick. "Now you know why I am not afraid. To know that God is watching over me is better than any breastplate."

"I wish I had armor like that," said one of the nobles.

"You may have it, you also may have it!" exclaimed Patrick joyfully. "Sing with me!"

The nobles quickly learned the words and the music of the new song and sang it all the way back to the castle. They called the song "Patrick's breastplate."

Patrick, meanwhile, went on his way rejoicing. The king sent his soldiers after him, but they could not find him.

For many years Patrick preached and taught in Ireland. Before his death in 461 he had founded over three hundred churches and baptized more than 120,000 persons. He came to be known as the one who "found Ireland all heathen and left it all Christian." Christ himself had called Patrick to this work and had opened the way for him.

What Can One Person Accomplish?

Telemachus

Telemachus was a monk who lived in Asia Minor about the year A.D. 400. During his life the gladiatorial games were very popular. The gladiators were usually slaves or political prisoners who were condemned to fight each other unto death for the amusement of the crowd. People were fascinated by the sight of spurting blood.

Telemachus was very much disturbed that the Christian Emperor Honorius sponsored these games and that so many people who called themselves Christians went to see them. What could be farther from the Spirit of Christ than the horrible cruelty of the gladiatorial games? The church was opposed to the games and spoke out against them, but most people would not listen.

Telemachus realized that talking about this evil was not enough. It was time to do something. But what could he accomplish—one lone monk against the whole Roman Empire? He was unknown. He had no power. And the games had been entrenched in Roman life for centuries. Nothing that he could possibly do would ever make a difference.

For a long time Telemachus agonized about the problem. Finally he could not live with himself any longer. For the integrity of his own soul he decided to obey Christ's Spirit within him, regardless of the consequences. He set out for Rome.

When Telemachus entered the city, the people he met had gone mad with excitement. "To the Colosseum! To the Colosseum! The games are about to begin!"

Telemachus followed the crowd. Soon he was seated among all the other people. Far away in a special place he saw the emperor.

The gladiators came out into the center of the arena. Everybody was tense. Everybody was quiet. Now the two strong young men drew their swords. The fight was on! One of them would probably die in a few minutes. Who would it be?

But just at that moment, Telemachus rose from his seat and ran into the arena. He held high the cross of Christ and threw himself between the two combatants.

"In the name of our Master," he cried, "stop fighting!"

The two men hesitated. Nothing like this had ever happened before. They did not quite know what to do.

But the spectators were furious. Telemachus had robbed them of their anticipated entertainment! They yelled wildly and stampeded toward the center of the arena. They became a mob. With sticks and stones they beat Telemachus to death.

Far down there in the arena lay the little battered body of the monk. Suddenly the mob grew quiet. A feeling of revulsion at what they had done swept over them. Emperor Honorius rose and left the Colosseum. The people followed him. Abruptly the games were over.

Honorius sensed the mood of the crowd and took this opportunity to issue an edict forbidding all future gladiatorial games.

So it was that in about the year A.D. 404, because one individual dared to say no, all gladiatorial games ceased.

The Vision of Sir Launfal
A Legend

Sir Launfal lay down on his bed. How he would ever fall asleep, however, he did not know. Tomorrow morning he was to leave his castle and ride out into the wide beautiful world! He had decided to search for the Holy Grail! How he hoped he would find it! It was the cup Jesus had used at the Last Supper and Sir Launfal knew that only a good and pure knight would ever be able to find it.

Now, was he all ready for the great adventure? Quickly Launfal reached out and tested his sword. Yes, it was sharp and he could see it gleaming in the moonlight. He would use that sword with great courage against anyone who dared to stop his search. Christ would be proud of him!

Over in the corner he saw his shield. It was polished and ready.

His horse, too, was ready. Launfal had personally fed him just before he went to bed.

Finally, Launfal fell asleep. He started dreaming. But his dream was so real that he thought it actually was morning and he was saying good-bye to all in the castle. Proudly he rode through the gates on his beautiful horse.

Just on the other side of the gates, however, a

beggar stopped him. How annoying! At this high moment when he was starting on his quest for the Holy Grail, he certainly could not be bothered with somebody as unimportant as a beggar. Disdainfully Sir Launfal flung a penny in his direction and rode on.

Time can pass very quickly in a dream. Sir Launfal dreamed that many years went by. He searched and searched for the Holy Grail. He fought many battles, but never did Christ even give him a glimpse of the cup which he had used at the Last Supper before his suffering and death.

Sir Launfal was discouraged. He had become an old man, and in his dream he finally decided to return home. Sadly he rode along in the wintry weather. As he came within sight of the castle, he saw all the lights ablaze, and he realized it was Christmas Eve. There would be much feasting and joy within the castle walls.

Sir Launfal rode up to the guard at the gate. To his dismay the guard did not recognize him. "No beggars allowed within the castle gates," he shouted rudely, and drove Launfal away.

In his dream, Sir Launfal got stiffly off his horse and sat down in the shelter of the castle wall. He looked at the light streaming out of the windows. Christmas Eve. The night the Christ Child was born, and he was excluded from his own home. Had Christ rejected him altogether?

Finally Sir Launfal pulled his last crust of bread from his pocket. Just as he was starting to eat it, he noticed a beggar nearby. Why, it was the same beggar that he had seen at the gates so many years ago as he was leaving on his mission! Sir Launfal broke his bread and gave half to the beggar. Then he went to the brook, broke the ice, and got some water for both of them to drink. As they ate together and drank from the old knight's wooden bowl, a strange thing happened. Suddenly Sir Launfal thought the crust of bread tasted like fresh bread and the water like the finest wine! He turned to the beggar. But the beggar was gone. In his place he saw the shining presence of Christ himself, and he heard Christ saying:

"Not what we give, but what we share, — For the gift without the giver is bare; Who gives himself with his alms feeds three, — Himself, his hungering neighbor, and me."

Sir Launfal looked down at his wooden bowl. It was no longer there either. Instead, he held in his hand the Holy Grail for which he had been searching these many years!

With that Sir Launfal woke from his sleep. It was morning. Launfal was deeply stirred by his dream. Christ had spoken to him and he knew what he must do.

"Put away my sword and armor," he instructed the servants. "I am not going to faraway countries to look for the Holy Grail. It is right here in my own castle."

From that day on, Sir Launfal opened wide the gates of his castle to the poor and hungry. He welcomed both rich and poor alike and was friendly to all. In his castle all experienced the love and kindness of one who had supped with Christ.

What Will Happen to Your Soul?

Baiko San

Baiko San lived in Japan. She was the wife of a Buddhist priest. They had never heard of Christ, but they lived according to the light that God had given them. No one who needed help was ever turned away from the little shrine where they lived. Baiko San and her husband had dedicated their lives to the service of others.

One day Baiko's husband died and she entered a monastery. But the villagers missed her so much that finally two of them came to see her.

"Baiko San," they said, "we have come to invite you in the name of our community to be our priest."

Baiko San was surprised. "I am a woman," she said. "How can I be your priest?"

"But you are the only priest we want," they said.

Baiko San thought a while and then she said, "Every morning I have turned my face in love toward the village where my husband's ashes are. Nothing would give me more joy than to live in that shrine and serve you."

So it was that Baiko San came back to live among the people she loved. No one thought that it was dangerous for her to live alone. Who would want to harm this woman who did everyone good and whom everyone loved? Baiko San was not afraid.

But one night Baiko woke up suddenly. Her mosquito net was moved by a human hand. The next moment a robber stood in front of her. The man had wrapped a towel around his face so she would not recognize him. Only his eyes were uncovered.

"Where did you put the money?" he asked roughly.

"What money?" asked Baiko San, surprised.

"There was a meeting here last night. They must have left an offering. I know it is hidden here somewhere. Don't try any tricks on me, old woman. See this sword?"

The robber thrust his sword through the mat at his feet. "That's what I'll do to you if you don't tell me," he hissed.

"Young man," said Baiko San calmly, "you can kill me with that sword of yours. But I have prayed for a long time now to be released from this body. I am ready. I want to go. But how about you? If you kill me, will it be well with *you*? What will happen to your soul? As for your body, you will be caught if you kill me. And then what? But I guess that is your worry, not mine.

"Now about the money. I saved some of the money people have given me. It is in the alcove there behind the altar. Just help yourself to it. I don't know about the other money. Good night."

Baiko San turned over and went to sleep.

Next morning it all seemed like a dream. But in the mat was the hole the sword had made. The money in the alcove, however, was undisturbed. The robber had not taken it. Baiko San had been a priest to him. He could not rob her.

Ashoka's Edict
A story of Ashoka, king of the Mauryan Empire

32   There is a story that happened many hundreds of years ago. The children in India hear it when they come to school. It goes something like this:

Young King Ashoka sat on his magnificent throne. Before him were assembled the generals of his army.

"My grandfather established this great Mauryan Empire," said the king.

The generals nodded.

"My father enlarged it."

The generals nodded again.

"My grandfather and my father both had a dream. They wanted to unite all of India under one rule. It falls to me, Ashoka, to make that dream come true!"

All of the generals bowed low before the king.

"As you know," continued Ashoka, "only Kalinga in the east and a little area in the south are still outside of our domain. It is our duty to conquer these people."

The generals all rose to their feet. "We are at your command," they called with one voice. "We are ready to go."

So it was that Ashoka's army suddenly descended on the people of Kalinga. These people were peacefully tending their farms. They were living their ordinary lives. Fathers and mothers were trying to bring up their children to be good men and women, kind to their friends, respectful to their elders, and obedient to the laws of their country. They had no idea that they were in any danger.

When Ashoka's soldiers stormed into their territory, the people of Kalinga fought hard, but they were no match for the imperial invaders.

Soon runners came back to King Ashoka with the news.

"Our soldiers are winning, O great King Ashoka!" cried the first messenger.

King Ashoka smiled proudly.

"One hundred thousand Kalingans have been killed on the battlefield," cried another messenger.

"One hundred thousand people slaughtered," repeated Ashoka, his eyes suddenly becoming thoughtful.

"More than a hundred thousand people are dying of their wounds," cried the third messenger.

King Ashoka's brows were wrinkled. "More than a hundred thousand people are dying of their wounds," he muttered to himself. Suddenly he could not stand thinking of the agony and the suffering of all these people. He turned away.

But already another messenger knelt before him, breathless with his news.

"Our troops have taken one hundred fifty thousand Kalingans as prisoners," he cried. "Your dream is coming true, O great Ashoka! Kalinga is ours."

But King Ashoka did not respond. Something was happening to him. The good news of Jesus, the Prince of Peace, had not reached him, but God was speaking to him in a powerful way. He heard God's voice and understood.

Once again King Ashoka sat on his magnificent throne. All the generals of his army, now drunk with victory, stood before him. They thought their king would send them out once more to conquer the last little bit of land to the south still missing from a great united India.

Instead, King Ashoka stood up and read the following edict: "I, King Ashoka, third king of the Mauryan Empire, herewith renounce all war and will henceforth practice a law of duty to

God."

The generals could not believe what they heard. At first they were speechless. Then one of them stepped forward and said, "We cannot understand your edict, O great Ashoka! The south is as good as in our hands. Why will you not fulfill the dream of your grandfather, your father, and your own to unite all India?"

"I am filled with remorse and disgust when I think of all the suffering and sorrow we have caused thousands of innocent people," said the king. "I do not want any more of that. From now I want to build a kingdom of peace, compassion, and love. It is wrong to kill or hurt any living creature."

Ashoka was true to his word. Without violence or bloodshed, the king set about to change India.

All along the roads of India he encouraged people to plant shade trees and orchards.

He began a tradition, which Indian villages still maintain, of providing rest houses for travelers.

He had his people dig wells, build hospitals, and provide relief for the needy.

The fine arts, especially drama, flourished.

Government officials were assigned to be peacemakers between any people who had a quarrel. Children were taught to listen to their parents, be respectful to their teachers, friendly and generous to all, and always to be kind to their servants.

Ashoka himself preached and taught throughout his kingdom what he practiced. And so it was that the great king was able to create one of the greatest models of social, economic, political, moral, spiritual, and aesthetic reconstruction of all times.

India became during his time an important international center, not through war but through love, peace, and concern for all people.

On the battlefield of Kalinga (now called Orissa) there still stands a carved stone on which is inscribed "Ashoka's 13th Edict" in which he renounced war. Historians say that Ashoka is the only monarch known to have abandoned war when he was so close to total military victory.

God Uses the Weak
Francis of Assisi

34

Francis of Assisi was sorely troubled. A great army of his Christian countrymen had come to Egypt to fight the Mohammedans. They were on a crusade to win the Holy Land from the Turks. They were killing many people. Francis saw people starving; he saw little children dying. It was not right. What could he do to stop the terrible massacre?

Francis decided to go to Cardinal Pelagius, the Christian commander of the army.

"Please, Lord Cardinal," he said, "stop the fighting. People are starving. People are dying without even having heard that Jesus loves them. And they are dying because of us Christians."

But Cardinal Pelagius would not listen. "We are killing these people for a good reason," he said. "We must conquer them so the church will be powerful. When the church is strong it will be able to conquer evil."

"The Lord Jesus did not ask us to strive for worldly power," replied Francis. "God uses the weak, not the powerful."

"Ridiculous!" cried Cardinal Pelagius angrily. He dismissed the poor man from Assisi without a further word.

Since the Christian commander would not listen to him, Francis decided to go to the enemy commander, the great Moslem Sultan Al-Kamil, to plead for peace. The Sultan was a cruel man. He had vowed that no Christian would ever leave his presence alive. But Francis was not afraid of him. Death would of course only bring him into the presence of his Lord.

Calmly Francis started out one morning walking toward the enemy camp.

The Sultan's soldiers did not take Francis seriously. He looked so small and so poor and unimportant in his threadbare cloak that they let him pass. When Francis smiled at them and asked, "Cairo? Al-Kamil? Soldan?" they just laughed and showed him the way to the Sultan's palace.

Just as Francis neared the gates of the palace, the Sultan, bedecked with jewels and followed by his retinue and crowds of people, came galloping down the road.

"Soldan! Soldan!" shouted Francis to attract his attention.

The foreign pronunciation of the word Sultan caught Al-Kamil's attention. As a ruler he had learned to speak Latin. He pulled his horse to an abrupt halt and looked at Francis with his piercing black eyes.

"Did you come from the Christian camp?" asked Al-Kamil.

"Yes, yes, I did," said Francis, smiling happily.

"I knew it!" cried the Sultan. He turned to his guards and said, "This fellow is a Christian!"

The guards, with daggers between their teeth, leaped upon Francis.

"Stop!" said the Sultan. "Don't kill him just yet. Bring him into the palace. I want to find out first what brought him here."

Soon Francis sat on the floor in front of the great Sultan.

"So!" exclaimed Al-Kamil, "did they send you over here to kill me?"

"Oh, no," said Francis. "No one sent me. I just came myself to ask you to end the war. Our commander won't listen to me, so I came to you."

The Sultan couldn't believe his ears. Nothing like this had ever happened to him before.

"What is your name, and where do you come from?" he asked.

"My name is Francis, and I came from the town

of Assisi in Italy," answered Francis.

"Well, Francis of Assisi, what do you want me to do?" asked the Sultan, amused. "Should I hand Egypt over to the enemy and let my people starve?"

"No," said Francis earnestly. "Egypt belongs to you. But you must do something else that would put an end to the war."

"What is that?" asked the Sultan.

"You must become a Christian," said Francis simply.

The Sultan broke into a gale of laughter. "Become a Christian!" he howled. "You know I will torture you, don't you? Aren't you afraid to suffer?"

"Our Lord suffered for us. Why should I not suffer for him?" said Francis.

"Your God suffered?" asked the Sultan, surprised.

"Yes, he suffered more than we can understand. He laid down his life for us. That is why we love him so much."

"Fair enough," said the Sultan, "but why should I love him when he did nothing for me?"

"Oh, but he did it for you, too," cried Francis. "He loves you. He knows you. You are his beloved child."

Francis spoke with such conviction that the Sultan became thoughtful. "What does your God require you to do?" he asked.

"Nothing, except that we love him," said Francis. "He wants us also to love everyone and share what we have with others."

"Ah," said the Sultan. "A long time ago we had a teacher in our midst who spoke about your faith as you do. But we have never found Christians to be like that. Christians are untruthful and cruel. They fight among themselves like wild animals. The stories about your faith are not true."

"Unfortunately there are evil Christians," said Francis. "Human nature is weak. But God's mercy has no limits. Through him the most wicked can become holy. That is not possible anywhere except in Christianity."

The Sultan sighed. "You may go now," he said. "I will not kill you. Indeed, I will even reward you for the interesting conversation I have had with you. Take all the gold you can carry."

"Gold!" exclaimed Francis, horrified. "I don't need gold."

"Well," said the Sultan, "that is the first time I have ever seen a Christian who does not want gold! What do you want then?"

"I would very much like to visit the Holy Land where our Lord lived when he was here on earth," said Francis. "Would you allow me to do so?"

A crafty look came into the Sultan's eyes. "Yes," he said. "I will even send a slave with you to take you as far as our borders. Remember, however, the slave belongs to me and you must send him back."

Francis nodded. "I will send him back," he said.

The Sultan turned to one of his guards. "Have one of the Christian slaves brought," he said. "He shall accompany this man to our border."

"But the slave will escape!" gasped the guard.

"Do as I tell you," shouted the Sultan. "We will see," he said to himself, "whether this Christian can be trusted. We will see whether he will send the slave back."

Francis and the Christian slave left the palace of the Sultan together.

– – – – – – – –

On many days the great Sultan Al-Kamil, with a wistful look in his eyes, asked his servants, "Has the slave that I sent with the Christian Francis of Assisi returned?"

"No, not yet, O great Ruler."

The Sultan stared out of the window. "I thought this man was different from the rest. I thought he was a real Christian. But I was wrong. They are all alike. All are false. All are untruthful. There is no such a person as a true Christian."

Just then a guard came in, bowing low. "Oh, great Ruler, I just want to report to you that the slave has returned," he said.

"Ah," said the Sultan. "So Francis of Assisi kept his word after all. Good! You may go."

Some time later, the Christian army was defeated. The commander, Cardinal Pelagius, who had hoped to make the church powerful, now stood in bitter humiliation before the Sultan, Al-Kamil. "Let our twelve thousand men go home," he begged.

"Listen to me," said the Sultan. "I vowed that not one of you Christians should remain alive. I would kill you all. Nothing you could say would have changed my mind. But some time ago a man by the name of Francis of Assisi came to me from your camp. I think highly of him."

Cardinal Pelagius looked up, startled. He vaguely remembered that foolish little man.

"He is the one and only man whose deeds showed me that the words about your faith are true," continued the Sultan. "For his sake, and for his sake alone, mind you, I will spare your lives. You may all go—you, as well as all my Christian slaves. I want Francis of Assisi to remember me well."

The Unbaptized Arm
Ivan the Great of Russia   1440-1505

Ivan the Great of Russia was a busy man. He was determined to free his country from the Tartars. That took a lot of planning and a lot of fighting. When he had accomplished that, he sat and poured over the law books. He knew they must be revised. And every day there were countless problems with the nobles and the church that he had to solve. Ivan of Russia had no time for himself.

"But this is not right," said his aides. "Our great ruler should get married and take some time out for family and friends. Otherwise he will be worn out before his time."

Cautiously they approached their ruler on the subject.

Ivan laughed. "Yes, you are right," he said. "I really should get married." Then he became serious. "Scout around for me among the ruling houses to see which princess would be a suitable wife for me."

Soon a delegation was sent out from Russia in search of a bride for Ivan, Grand Duke of Moscovy. They searched far and wide and finally decided to recommend Sophia, the daughter of the king of Greece.

Ivan was satisfied with the choice. He asked the king of Greece for his daughter in marriage.

"Yes," said the king, "I shall be glad to give you my daughter in marriage, but there is one condition."

"What is that?" asked Ivan.

"You must become a member of the Greek Orthodox Church," answered the king of Greece.

"Why, of course, of course," said Ivan. "It makes no difference to me which church I belong to. I shall be glad to join Sophia's church."

"Very good," replied the king. "I shall send you a priest to instruct you on how to become a Christian."

Now this is where Ivan's problems began. First of all, he found out that he had to be baptized. That was not so bad. He felt he could put up with that. But then the priest gave him the requirements for baptism. One of the articles stated that a member of the Christian church could not be a soldier!

"What!" roared Ivan. "I can't fight anymore?"

"No," said the priest. "Christians do not carry arms. They follow Christ, the Prince of Peace."

"Well, well, well," said Ivan. He was used to solving problems. Surely he could marry Sophia and still do as he pleased.

The priests of the Greek Orthodox Church made their plans for the baptism of Ivan the Great of Russia.

Ivan the Great of Russia also made his plans. He thought he had found a solution to his problem.

On the day of the baptism, Ivan and five hundred of his soldiers came to the body of water where the baptism was to take place. It had been decided that the army should also be baptized. Five hundred priests stood ready to perform the baptism.

Together, they went into the water. But lo and behold, as Ivan and his soldiers were immersed, each held his right arm with the sword high above the water. The fighting arms and the swords were left unbaptized!

So it was that Ivan the Great became a member of the Christian church, married the princess of Greece, and kept right on fighting!

37

How Did God Conquer Your Heart?

Mouttet, 1495

A long, long time ago in the fifteenth century lived a man by the name of Mouttet. He and his family and friends were farmers in one of the valleys of the Savoy Mountains in France. Their ancestors had come to this hidden valley many years before because they had been persecuted by the church. They had preached about Jesus Christ in the people's own language at a time when the church thought it must be done only in Latin.

The people in the little valley now thought they were safe. Their farm was surrounded by high mountain crags and could only be reached through a narrow passageway which led into the valley from the east. They had armed themselves well and constantly guarded the narrow entrance to their valley. If the enemy should try to force their way in, they could easily defend it.

Mouttet and his people did not rely on their swords alone, however. Daily they prayed to God that he might protect them. And daily they studied the Bible. They tried very hard to be obedient to God in everything they did. They called themselves "The Fellowship of the Cross."

One day in the fall while Mouttet was busy with the harvest, a young man came running up to him in great haste.

"Father Mouttet!" he called, all out of breath. "I have just come from the pass in the mountains."

"Are the enemy soldiers trying to get in again?" asked Mouttet.

"No, no," gasped the man. "They have closed the entrance from the outside! We cannot get out!"

Mouttet called all his friends and neighbors together.

"It is obvious that the enemy plans to starve us out," he said. "What shall we do?"

"For the time being, we are safe," said one man. "We have just put in a good supply of everything we need for the winter."

"We must be very careful with the food," said another. "Perhaps the enemy will leave before it runs out. But in any case let us make sure that we all have swords ready if they should attack."

"Yes," said Mouttet. "And now let us pray that God might deliver us from our enemies."

The whole congregation knelt down to pray and then rose from their knees with new faith and confidence. Surely God would intervene! Surely God would show them how to save their homes!

During the winter all went fairly well. But in early spring, the supplies began to run low. Some of Mouttet's men were good mountain climbers and knew of a hidden path to the west. It was very dangerous but from time to time they could sneak out and bring in some supplies. They could not bring in enough, however. The people were starving. It seemed that they would have to give up!

If they surrendered to the enemy they would be killed. There was the hidden passage to the west, but the spring avalanches would begin at any time, and they might all be buried by them if they took that route. What should they do? Mouttet was deeply disturbed. Had God not heard their prayers? Had he forgotten them?

One evening they all met together. Again they prayed to God and committed their lives to him. Then they silently went out into the pitch-dark night. They would try to get out across the mountains in the west.

As they entered the rocky passageway, the spring winds howled through the clefts. However, no avalanche came down. The men, women, and children moved forward, sad and discouraged. They could not understand why God had permitted the enemy to drive them from their beloved valley.

The morning after Mouttet's people had left through the western passage, the enemy snipers in the mountains noticed that no smoke rose from the chimneys of the houses. Cautiously they went to investigate. The farm was deserted. The Fellowship of the Cross had fled!

Soon the whole army swarmed over the place. They found the tracks the Mouttet group had left and followed them. Soon they too stood at the entrance to the hidden passageway. They all knew about the dangerous avalanches, but one officer shouted, "What they did, we can do also!" So in they went! But before they had advanced many steps, a terrible rumbling began. They tried to turn back, but with a roar the avalanche was upon them. They were buried alive.

The Fellowship of the Cross found refuge in different places in Switzerland. Mouttet and his family were taken in by people at the foot of the Saintes Mountain and were soon able to support themselves.

Here, in their new home, Father Mouttet gathered his family about him each evening and read from the Bible. Over and over again he asked the question that troubled all of them: *Why* had God permitted all this to happen? Had they not honestly tried to serve him? They believed that God could have helped them and given them victory over their enemies. Why had

he not done so?

One night as Mouttet again searched his Bible trying to find the answer, his wife came and put her arm around his shoulders. "How did the Lord overcome your heart when you were converted to him?" she asked. "Was it by fire and sword?"

"What foolish talk!" Mouttet replied. "It was his mercy and unspeakable love that conquered my stubborn, evil heart."

"And did God not tell us to be his witnesses?" his wife asked.

"And did we not witness for him?" asked Mouttet in return.

"Do you think we can tell others about the love of God with swords and weapons?" she insisted.

Mouttet looked at his wife in amazement. This was a new thought to him, and he did not know what to say.

"Jesus showed human beings the Father's love by dying on the cross," continued his wife. "Perhaps he chose to let us suffer that we might also tell others of his love and not persecute and kill our enemies as they persecute and kill us."

A sparkle came into the old man's eyes. His wife had found the answer to his questions. A deep peace entered his mind and filled his heart.

Many years later Christians were again severely persecuted. In the region of Switzerland where Mouttet had lived and witnessed, a group of people called "Children of Peace" did not defend themselves. They died to tell others of God's love, rather than kill their enemies with the sword.

Free to Love

Michael Sattler   1490-1527

40   Michael Sattler heaved a sigh of relief as he packed together the various notes and papers he had used in presiding over the Schleitheim Conference. He was glad it was over. But he was also glad that it had taken place. Participants had been able to agree on seven articles of faith. Now the new Anabaptist congregations in Switzerland and South Germany, floundering around in so many new teachings, would have something to go by. Michael carefully tucked the piece of paper on which the seven articles of faith were written into his inner suit pocket. He must guard it well so it would not get into enemy hands.

And then, after shaking hands with many dear brethren, he was on his way home to Horb. Michael smiled as he mounted his horse. He would soon see his wife again and tell her about everything that had happened in Schleitheim. How good it was to have a companion with whom he could share his thoughts and concerns and dreams! He thought of his lonely life as a monk in the monastery before he had become an Anabaptist. How wonderfully God had guided his life since then! He and his wife were able to guide many people into a new fellowship of faith. Of course it all had to be in secret since the government did not recognize this faith.

Michael urged his horse to a faster trot. And then finally, late at night, he was in front of his own house in Horb. There was a candle in one of the windows. His wife was waiting for him!

Quickly he took his horse to the barn and bounded up the steps. His wife opened the door and drew him in.

"Michael," she whispered, "close the door quickly. I think we are being watched."

"Why? What has happened?"

"The Anabaptists in Rottenburg have been discovered!"

Michael Sattler sat down heavily. He knew what this meant. They both knew. Michael and his wife were prominent leaders of the Anabaptist movement. Since the authorities had some clues now, they would surely find them very soon. Of course they had always realized that this hour would come. They had shared their faith with others, fully realizing the danger of doing it against the law of the land. But they had committed their lives to God in Christ and had experienced the joy of his presence and blessing. Why would he forsake them now? In their hour of terrible need they turned to God and were not disappointed. A deep peace filled their souls.

"Whatever happens," murmured Michael before they fell asleep, "we must not let fear and hate take possession of us. God is love, and if he fills our hearts we too will be free to love."

A few days after Michael's return home, the soldiers were at their door. They burst rudely into the house and grabbed Michael. First they searched all his pockets.

"Ha," they shouted. "Look here! All the evidence we need!" Quickly the paper with the seven points drawn up at the Schleitheim Conference were torn from Michael and given to the man in charge. Then Michael and his wife were taken to prison.

Already many other men and women were there. And more and more were brought in until the prison at Horb could not hold them all. Many, many people in that area had confessed their Lord and Master in believer's baptism and were now being rounded up.

Since the Anabaptists were well liked by their neighbors, the authorities did not trust the citizens in the town of Horb. Michael Sattler was especially loved and respected. The people in Horb might revolt. Some of the officials saddled fourteen horses and took Michael Sattler and his wife and several others to a prison in a little town called Binsdorf.

Here they were kept for almost three months while the trial was being prepared. Michael wrote to the congregation at Horb. He tried to comfort them. He knew that martyrdom awaited him. But he encouraged them to be steadfast.

The trial opened on May 17, 1527, in Rottenburg. Michael and his wife, together with twelve other men and women, were accused, among other things, of disobeying the law of the land. The Catholic church was the only legal one in the empire at that time. This church they had abandoned. So they were charged with committing not only a religious crime, but also a civil one. Michael was also accused of not being willing to bear arms against the enemy.

Michael Sattler spoke for the whole group. Even though they were treated with rudeness and great cruelty, Michael remained courteous and calm. "Ye ministers of God," he addressed his judges, "If you have neither heard nor read the Word of God, we would suggest that you send for the most learned men and for the Book of the divine Scriptures, and that they with us weigh these things in the light of the Word of God. If they show us from Holy Scripture that we err and are in the wrong, we shall be gladly taught, and recant."

But the officer who represented the state said angrily, "The only one who will have a discussion with you will be the executioner!"

The judges left the room, leaving Sattler to the jeering soldiers. After an hour and thirty minutes the judges returned with the verdict. It read as follows:

"Between the representatives of his Imperial Majesty and Michael Sattler judgment is passed that Michael Sattler shall be delivered to the executioner, who shall firstly cut out his tongue, then throw him upon a cart and with red hot tongs tear pieces out of his body twice, and on the way to the place of execution make use of the tongs five times more in like manner. Thereupon he shall burn his body to ashes as an arch heretic."

Even when Michael heard this terrible sentence, he did not lose his composure. Christ had freed him from fear and hate and had given him his love. On the morning of his execution, Michael Sattler prayed for his judges and persecutors and admonished the people to repent. Then the sentence was carried out.

When the fire burned through the cords with which he was bound, Michael lifted up the two forefingers of his hand. It was the sign he had promised to his friends to show that he was steadfast to the end and endured it all willingly for Christ!

Sattler's wife was drowned a few days later. She also remained faithful to the end. Both of them had kept their hearts free to love.

Never Again

Christian Mueller

About the time Columbus made his third trip to America, a boy called Christian Mueller was born in the Black Forest of Germany.

There was much unrest in Germany during the time when Christian was growing up. In 1517 Martin Luther tacked his ninety-five theses on the church door in Wittenberg to challenge the Roman Catholic church to look at some of its practices. The peasants or farmers were finally fed up with the oppression they experienced by the church and by the wealthy. They revolted.

Young Christian was right in there. His uncle, Hans Mueller, became a famous leader in the peasant revolt. How Christian admired him! Uncle Hans saw how the Catholic church exploited the people. Uncle Hans would help to bring about justice and prosperity for them. With all his heart Christian wanted to be a part of this great movement.

When he was old enough, Christian, too, led a group of angry farmers, as they stormed across the country, burning homes and barns, stealing livestock, and killing those who remained loyal to the Catholic church. Sometimes all the violence and cruelty sickened Christian. But Uncle Hans felt it was necessary to destroy the oppressors before a new world could be born. Uncle Hans spoke convincingly, and Christian believed him.

One day when Christian and his group of peasants were sacking and looting a Catholic village, Christian entered one of the houses. It was empty. "The family must be hiding," he thought to himself. He ordered his men to surround the place while he and a companion searched all the buildings.

Finally when Christian came to the barn, he stopped short. There, on the floor of the stable, knelt an old man. His white hair fell down over his shoulders. In his hands he held high a small wooden crucifix, and even when Christian entered, he calmly continued to pray.

As Christian stood silently for a moment, his companion rushed in through the door, lifted his long sword, and with a single swift blow struck off the old man's head. The white head, smeared with its own blood, rolled near Christian's feet. He looked for a moment at the calm staring eyes which seemed to gaze at him from the bodiless head.

With that, something happened within Christian. He saw clearly what he had been doing. And in that instant, he grasped his own sword, crashed it against his upraised knee, and broke the steel blade in two.

Throwing away the pieces, Christian said in a calm strong voice to his companions who had gathered in the stable, "Never again will these hands of mine wield a sword."

The news that Christian had deserted them spread like wildfire through the ranks of revolting peasants. They were furious. Christian had to flee for his life.

Where could he hide? In the neighboring village there was a group of Anabaptists. Since they believed bloodshed was wrong, they had not participated in the revolt. Here Christian found temporary refuge. And these people also gave him letters of introduction to the Anabaptists in Switzerland and helped him to escape to the canton of Berne.

In Berne, Christian Mueller became a leader of the Anabaptists, later called *Mennonites*. He kept the promise that he had made in that moment of decision. Never again did he wield a sword, even in the cause of justice.

Following the Prince of Peace
Menno Simons

Menno Simons, the Catholic priest in Witmarsum, Holland, was sitting at the desk in his study when there was an urgent knock at his door.

"Come in!" he called, and at the same time jumped up to let his caller in.

It was a woman of his parish. "Father!" she gasped. "Father!"

Menno led her to a chair for she seemed so distraught, she could hardly stand.

"What is the matter? What has happened?" he asked her.

"My son, my son Hendrick—you know, don't you, that after Jan van Geelen was here, that Hendrick joined the Anabaptists?"

Menno Simons nodded.

"Well, Jan van Geelen told us we would not get anywhere with our new faith if we just sit back and allow ourselves to be killed. He thinks we should arm ourselves and conquer the whole province of Friesland. Then we would be in a position to spread the good news of Jesus Christ. Hendrick believed him and went with him and now—" Hendrick's mother started crying heartbrokenly.

Menno Simons waited until she could speak again.

"Three hundred men and women went with Jan van Geelen. Last week they seized the old monastery, the Oldeklooster near Bolsward—"

Menno Simons nodded again. He had heard the news, but had not talked to anyone about it. He had to be so extremely careful.

"And yesterday, yesterday—" Hendrick's mother sobbed again— "the imperial army bombarded the monastery and killed almost everyone. Hendrick is dead. And several others from our congregation are also dead!"

Menno Simons started in shocked surprise.

"Who brought this news?" he asked.

"Jan van Geelen escaped, and he told someone to come and tell us. But the man does not want us to mention his name."

"Of course," said Menno Simons.

After Hendrick's mother was gone, Menno Simons sank down in his chair again and covered his face with his hands. Then he reached for the Bible he had in his drawer and poured over its pages. The Bible had become his authority. After a while he looked up and said, "No! No! No! It is wrong. Following in the footsteps of the Prince of Peace who shed his blood for all of us alike, we must do *good* to those that hate us. We cannot kill them. Jesus said, 'He who takes up the sword, shall perish by the sword.' That is as true now as it was then."

Menno Simons looked out into the spring evening, heavy with blossoms. A bird was singing, but he did not hear it. He walked restlessly back and forth.

"But what have I done to prevent this tragedy at the Oldeklooster?" he asked himself. "The people who followed Jan van Geelen didn't know the Scriptures. And I didn't teach them the way of the Lord, even though I knew it. But I was afraid, afraid to come into the open. I was afraid of the persecution. I was afraid to suffer with my Lord."

Menno paused a while in deep thought. Then he murmured, "—And I am still afraid!"

Some time after the massacre at the Oldeklooster, a friend of Menno's came to talk to him in his study.

"Menno," he said, "you must do something. Jan van Leyden, who you know has abandoned the peaceful principles of the Anabaptist teaching, has been named king of the 'New Jerusalem.' He is setting up in Muenster, and is recruiting followers around here. He wants us to come to Muenster to serve in his army. He says we must help Christ usher in the millennium and that we, the believers, will execute judgment on the unbelievers. We will take revenge and destroy them."

Menno shook his head sadly. "I am afraid Jan has faith in his own visions and feelings instead of in the Lord Jesus Christ. He thinks if he prays hard enough and believes hard enough, God will do what he wants. Jan van Leyden is forgetting to check out his dreams with the Scriptures. The two don't agree. Christ did not usher in his kingdom with military might—he ushered it in on the cross. And he did so when he could have called on more than twelve legions of angels to defend him. Christ would not allow Peter to defend him with the sword. How can a Christian then defend himself with it?"

"I am glad to hear you say that so clearly, Menno, but how are we to sort all this out when we don't know the Scriptures? It is so hard when more and more of our loved ones are dying a martyr's death. Then the thought that we should defend them and save them from torture seems good and right. Deep down, I know that is not the way to bring in Christ's kingdom. Menno, write down where Jan van Leyden is wrong so we can pass it around for people to read who don't know what to do."

"Yes," said Menno. "I will start writing immediately."

So Menno wrote a pamphlet called "The Blasphemy of Jan van Leyden." But before it was even published something happened.

In July of the same year that the people in the Oldeklooster were defeated, Jan van Leyden and his followers were defeated in Muenster. The "New Jerusalem" he had believed in so passionately was gone. Instead, Jan and many, many of the people whom he had led astray were killed.

Now Menno Simons could stand it no longer. He preached from the Bible much more openly and talked freely to individual people, even though he knew it was very dangerous. He could no longer believe what the Bible said, and act as if he knew nothing about it. He felt responsible for the people who had been touched by the faith in Jesus Christ but who were like sheep without a shepherd. Menno Simons was no longer afraid.

He spoke openly as long as he could, but early in 1536 it became clear that he would be arrested if he stayed in his church. Quietly one night he slipped away. His good position and salary, his comfortable home and professional friends could no longer hold him. He was ready to follow wherever Christ would lead him.

And so it was that Christ sent Menno Simons, a fugitive, out to gather the many people who were hungry for the Word of God at that time. Menno preached, he taught, he counseled. Now the community of believers could together follow the Prince of Peace.

44

Violence Absorbed

Elizabeth Dirks

Early one morning, just as the sun was rising, a young milkmaid came out of the convent Tienge near Leer in East Friesland. She was a trim young maid, and she swung her milk pail as if she loved going out into the fresh young morning to milk. Not far away in the pasture the cows were waiting for her.

But the cows stood and stared in dumb astonishment. When the milkmaid went right through their midst and kept on walking, the cows stared after her and moo-ooed quietly. At that the maid turned around, her eyes laughing, and said, "You're right. I am not the real one. But don't you tell a soul!"

Elizabeth Dirks was indeed not the real milkmaid. She was a young nun who was escaping from the convent. The milkmaid, who was her friend, had given Elizabeth some of her clothes so no one watching from the convent would suspect her. Once Elizabeth was through the cow pasture and into the woods, she walked swiftly and quietly. Her laughing eyes had become serious, and her face was strained. She must get to Leer before anyone would miss her at the convent.

Elizabeth had secretly been studying the Bible for many years and had decided to break with the Catholic church. In the city of Leer she knew an Anabaptist family who would hide her.

As Elizabeth walked, she prayed. "God," she said, "I know this is dangerous. I know I might not live long. But I want my life, even if it is short, to be worthwhile. I want to help build your kingdom. Please show me the way."

In Leer, Elizabeth's friends were overjoyed to see her. It was very difficult, however, to keep her hidden for any length of time. Always the

government and church officials were on the lookout for heretics. Since Elizabeth had escaped from the convent there was a special search for her.

At one of the secret meetings in the woods, a woman said, "I know a woman in Leeuwarden who I am sure would be very glad to have Lysken live with her. Her name is Hadewyk (Hait-duh-vike), and she lives alone. Her husband had to flee because he showed sympathy for Sike Freerks when he was executed for his faith. Hadewyk has now become an Anabaptist Christian."

After some discussion, it was decided that they would secretly take Elizabeth to Leeuwarden. How Elizabeth hoped that God would have something for her to do in that city!

Sure enough, soon after Hadewyk had welcomed her with open arms, Menno Simons came to Leeuwarden and visited Hadewyk. During the conversation Menno said, "We are planning to have a secret meeting tonight, but there are some people who don't know where to leave their little children."

Elizabeth jumped up. "Please," she cried, "could I take care of them? Hadewyk, may they bring them here?"

Menno and Hadewyk both smiled. "Of course," said Hadewyk, "if you really want to do that, Lysken. I am sure the parents will be greatly relieved."

That is how Elizabeth's work started. She loved the children, and the children loved her. Soon she was a good friend of the parents. Wherever she went, she sang, and her merry laugh and smiling eyes were like a ray of sunshine in a dark world. People knew they could trust her. They knew she would understand. They knew she

would have compassion with them. And when they had questions about their newfound faith in Christ, Elizabeth could help them find the answers. Menno Simons soon relied very heavily on her to visit the sick and the bereaved and the sorrowful.

"Lysken," Menno said to her one day when he was in Leeuwarden, "what would we do without you? You are the deaconess of this secret congregation just as Phoebe was in the early church."

Elizabeth's face beamed. "Thank you, Menno," she said. "I am glad that Christ had work for me here. It has made my life rich and free. Even if it should not last long, it will have been worth it."

Soon someone in the town sensed that Elizabeth and Hadewyk, who were always ready to help everyone, must be Anabaptists. They spied on them. And on January 15, 1549, both Elizabeth and Hadewyk were arrested and taken to jail.

They were put into separate cells. After a while Hadewyk's cell door was opened at night in a mysterious way and she could escape. But Elizabeth had to stay in jail and was called before the magistrates.

"Are you an Anabaptist?" they asked her.

"Yes," she said calmly. "I believe in the Lord Jesus Christ, and I have been baptized upon the confession of my faith."

"And this you did even though you knew that it is against the law to be baptized again?"

"I know it is against your laws, but I obey a higher law—the command of Christ," Elizabeth said.

"How did you come to believe in this heresy?" asked the presiding priest.

"I came to know of the great love of the Lord Jesus Christ for me through reading the Scriptures," answered Elizabeth.

"There you have it," said the priest angrily. "If we could only keep the people from reading the Bible. It does unending harm!"

"Are there others who have been studying the Bible with you?" asked the magistrate with a crafty look on his face.

"Yes," said Elizabeth simply.

"Who are they?"

"That I will not tell you," said Elizabeth firmly.

"Ah, so!" said the magistrate. "We shall soon help you to tell us. See these thumbscrews? They will squeeze your thumbs until you will be glad to remember who your heretic friends are."

Elizabeth closed her eyes. "Lord, help me!" she prayed. The terrible torture was applied until the blood spurted from her thumbs. But the love of Christ surrounded Elizabeth like a great cloud so that she could bear the pain.

"Are you willing to talk now?" asked the magistrate.

Elizabeth looked at the cruel magistrate with deep suffering eyes. "Your violence to another human being is a slap in the face of our Creator. I will not allow that violence to be done to my friends as well. I shall absorb the violence. It shall stop with my body."

The authorities of Leeuwarden kept Elizabeth in jail for several months, trying in vain to break down her resistance, but finally she was condemned to death. On May 27, 1549, Elizabeth Dirks was drowned.

Her short life on earth was over, but her prayer that day when she escaped as a little milkmaid had been answered. Her life had been worthwhile!

Blessed Are the Merciful

Menno Simons

Christmas 1553 had almost come to Wismar, a city on the north shore of Germany. Big beautiful snowflakes had transformed the peaked roofs, the walls, and the bare trees into a white wonderland before it turned very cold.

Lottie and Hans looked out the window of their playroom on the third floor of their house. They could see the harbor from there.

"Look, Hans," cried Lottie suddenly. "Over there! Can you see a ship?"

"Where, where?" said Hans, pressing his nose against the cold pane.

Soon Hans located the ship, too. It was moving very, very slowly. Excitedly the children rushed downstairs to tell their mother. At the noon meal the ship in the harbor was the main topic of conversation.

"It seems the ship is from England and it is now pretty well stuck in the ice," said Mr. Mueller, the children's father. "I heard that the port authorities are trying to get out to it and see what can be done."

"But why would a ship venture out here at this time of winter?" asked Menno Simons, the Anabaptist preacher who was staying as a guest with the family.

"It does seem strange," said Mr. Mueller. "They should have known better."

Before nightfall Mr. Mueller had found out that the ship was filled with refugees. They were Dutch people who belonged to the Reformed church and who had settled in England. Now they were trying to escape from England where they were cruelly persecuted because they did not believe everything the Catholic church taught.

"There are men, women, and children on board," said Mr. Mueller at the supper table, "and they are all sitting there in that drafty old boat in this weather. They will freeze to death!"

"Why can't they come ashore?" cried Lottie.

"They could walk across the ice," said Hans. "We skated there yesterday and the ice is solid."

"Those people can't come ashore because the town fathers of Wismar won't let them," said Mr. Mueller in disgust.

"What?" everybody around the table cried in disbelief.

"Yes, that is what I said—they will not allow the people to come into the city because Wismar believes what Luther preaches and the freezing people on the boat believe what John Calvin preaches."

"Then we must do what Menno Simons preaches," said Mrs. Mueller with determination.

"Thank you, my dear," said Menno Simons, smiling, "but let us change that to 'We must do what the Bible teaches.'"

"What do you mean?" asked Lottie and Hans in one breath.

"Jesus said, 'Blessed are the merciful, for they shall obtain mercy,' and that means that we must help these people without delay," said Menno Simons. "How can this best be done?"

Mr. and Mrs. Mueller looked at each other.

"I heard that they are completely out of food," said Mr. Mueller. "The first thing we must do is bring them some food, and then we shall see how we can help them get into the city for shelter."

"I'll get all the bread and cheese we have in the house, and Lottie and Hans can help me pack the food," said Mrs. Mueller. Then she turned to her husband. "The Webers and the Schroeders down the street will also want to help."

"I'll go immediately and describe the situation to them," said her husband.

"And I'll go to the Funks," said Menno Simons. "I know them."

"Yes," said Mrs. Mueller, "and they can go to the other Anabaptists in their part of town."

It did not take very long until the whole Mueller family, together with Menno Simons and some of their friends, were on their way across the ice to the ship. They carried food and also some blankets.

There on the small, old sailing vessel sat the refugees all huddled together. They were hungry and cold. When Menno Simons and the other people with him stepped on board, their minister and leader, Herman Bakereel came to meet them.

"What is this?" said Herman Bakereel. "Who are you?"

"We are your friends," said Menno. "In the name of the Lord Jesus Christ we want to help you."

"But do you know that we are of the Reformed church and that this city won't let us land?"

"Yes, we know," said Menno. "But the Scriptures teach us to help those who are hungry. We care about you. Will you accept this food and the blankets from our hands?"

"Yes, yes," said Herman Bakereel, almost moved to tears in his distress for his people. "We thank you for your help. At least tonight our children will not go hungry."

"Tomorrow morning we shall see whether we can get permission to take you to our homes until your situation can be settled," said Mr. Mueller.

And so it was that in that Christmas season every Anabaptist family in the city of Wismar had guests. Lottie and Hans played in the snow with Ada and Jan, the Dutch children from England. And when Christmas Eve came, they shared their toys with them.

On Christmas day the Anabaptists had a secret service in one of their homes to which they invited their guests. Menno Simons read the Christmas story from Luke 2. When he came to the phrase "because there was no place for them in the inn," Herman Bakereel murmured, "There was no place for our Lord, but you have made room for us, the homeless, on the night of his birth. We thank you for that!"

The Reformed refugees that the Anabaptists had befriended were soon banned from Wismar and went to Luebeck. But Lottie and Ada and Hans and Jan remained friends and always remembered the beautiful Christmas they spent together in Wismar when they were children.

A Stain and Burden on Our Conscience
The Hutterian Brethren

That day in 1579 began like any other. The sun rose. The people—grandparents, parents, and children—in the communities of the Hutterian Brethren in Moravia rose to do their daily tasks. But then something happened. A messenger came galloping down the road! He dismounted and gave the leader of the community a letter.

Somehow everybody sensed that it was something serious. And sure enough, very soon the whole community was called together and the letter was read. It was from the governing lord of that area, and it said that the Hutterian Brethren would need to pay a tax to finance a war in which the country was engaged.

"As you know, we have always been nonresistant," said the leader of the Brethren to his people. "We have never gone to war because Christ taught us to love our enemies. Now we are asked to pay a war tax. This is something new. What shall we do?"

The whole assembly was quiet for a long time. Their leader knew they were all praying and asking God for guidance.

Then one person said, "We must be true to our Lord. If we love our enemies, we cannot kill them."

"But we would not be killing our enemies if we pay the war tax," said another. "We would just be doing our duty as citizens of this country. We would be obeying the Word as it is written in Romans 13:6 and 7: "For the same reason you also pay taxes, for the authorities are ministers of God, attending to this very thing. Pay all of them their dues, taxes to whom taxes are due, revenue to whom revenue is due, respect to whom respect is due, honor to whom honor is due.""

"But the same Word admonishes us in chapter 12 to feed our enemy and give him to drink. How can we do that and at the same time kill him?"

asked a person in the back of the room.

"We are not talking about killing our enemies," said a man curtly. "We are talking about paying taxes."

"And what difference is there between killing a person and paying someone else to do it?" retorted a young person heatedly.

"Let us be calm and listen what the Spirit of the Lord tells us," interrupted their leader.

Everybody bowed their heads. There was another long silence. Then the man who had spoken about doing their duty as citizens said brokenly, "I said what I said because I am afraid of the consequences. We have had so much persecution. If we refuse to pay the tax, what will happen to us?"

"That is not the question to ask," said another gently. "The question is what followers of the Prince of Peace should do."

There was a murmur of assent.

And so it was that the Hutterian Brethren decided to refuse to pay the war tax which was laid on them. They sent a messenger to the authorities explaining why they could not pay for war. The little community knew that their disobedience to the government would have painful consequences. But they slept that night, glad that they had not participated willingly in evil.

The authorities did not look kindly on the decision of the Hutterian Brethren. They seized and confiscated some of their property, such as cattle or sheep, to cover the sum asked for war taxes.

In spite of what happened, the chronicler of the Brethren writes, "We suffer the spoiling of our goods (Hebrews 10:34) rather than do that which would be a stain and burden on our conscience."

The White Feather

Sebulon Hoxie and Norbert Nisbet

The people in the little Quaker settlement in the state of New York were very uneasy. It was the year 1775 and there was much talk about a war between the colonies and Great Britain. Besides that, the Indians were on the warpath because the government had broken its promise to them once again. They wanted revenge.

Even though the authorities had advised the settlers to leave the area until a more peaceful time should come, the Quakers had stayed in their homes. They believed that fleeing from the situation was not the answer. They wanted to be friends with the Indians. They wanted to live fairly and peacefully with them. They believed that they must trust God to guide and protect them.

But still the people in the little Quaker settlement could not help being afraid. They heard of the terrible raids. They knew that many people were killed. What would happen to them, all alone there in the woods?

The days went by slowly. As yet all was peaceful and quiet. The Quakers went about their work as usual. When Sunday came, they all went to their meetinghouse for the morning service.

There a surprise awaited them! Beside their leader, Sebulon Hoxie, sat the great Quaker, Norbert Nisbet. Norbert Nisbet had walked through the dense forest for two days to be with them. Oh, surely Norbert Nisbet would have a word from the Lord for them!

When Norbert Nisbet arose to speak, all eyes were fixed on him. He read Deuteronomy 33:12: "The Lord's beloved dwells in security, the High God shields him all the day long, and he dwells under his protection."

After reading this word, he said, "You have done well, my friends, that you have stayed in your homes when all your neighbors have fled. That is why I have come to you. I wanted to assure you that God cares about you and that he will protect you. Believe this word and you need not fear the arrow that flies by day, for 'he will cover you with his pinions, and you shall find safety beneath his wings'" (Psalm 91:4).

After Norbert Nisbet had spoken, the customary silence descended on the people in the meetinghouse. They communed with God, each in his or her heart. The little children fell asleep on their mothers' laps. The older children looked through the cracks between the logs where they could see into the forest.

But what was that? The children's hearts almost stopped! Clearly through the leaves they saw blue, red, and yellow feathers flash here and there and then disappear. The branches of the trees swayed back and forth although there was not a breeze anywhere. And then, almost immediately, Indians in full war paint, with their arrows drawn, appeared in the side openings of the meetinghouse. In the door at the back stood the Indian chief with several associates, also completely armed.

Horror rippled through the congregation. However, even though their faces became pale and their bodies trembled, not a single person in the room moved. They were used to silent concentration.

The Indian chief looked suspiciously around the room for weapons, but there were none. He gave his warriors a signal—they took their arrows from their bows and stuck them into their holders.

Then the Indian chief looked at Grandfather Hoxie. With sure instinct he knew that this was the "white chief." For a long time he looked directly at him. Grandfather Hoxie returned the look calmly. Two powerful men tested each other's strength. On the face of the Indian there was the expression of cold disdain. Too often and too long had the white man shamefully deceived him! On Grandfather Hoxie's face there was, even in this hour of terrible concern for his people, a reflection of that love with which Christ had flooded his heart.

Finally the Indian chief looked down. Strange, this white man had no weapons and yet was clearly not afraid. The Indian chief signaled to his men. They all laid down their bows and arrows and came into the meetinghouse. Thirteen Indians sat down on the benches with the white people.

The service continued as before—in complete silence. It was the most memorable service the Quakers had ever had. They all felt that the Spirit of God was there and that the words "You shall find safety beneath his wings" were a living reality. But not only the Quakers were quiet. The Indians, too, were completely silent. They seemed to feel at home in this circle of worshipers.

When the service was over, the two leading Quakers shook hands, and then Grandfather Hoxie walked over to the Indian chief. He invited him and his warriors to his house for a simple meal. They understood the invitation and accepted it.

In the Hoxie home they all ate bread and butter and cheese together.

Then the Indian chief spoke. Norbert Nisbet could interpret his words. The chief said, "We came to kill you. But when we saw you sitting here so quietly without any weapons, we lost all desire to harm you. And now we shall protect you, for we feel that you worship the Great Spirit that is also in us."

After he had said that, the Indian chief took an arrow with a white feather out of his quiver and fastened it over the door outside. "This feather will protect you from any attacks by the Indians," he explained. "From now on, the Indians are your friends."

52

The Cheyenne Way of Peace

Sweet Medicine

A long, long time ago the Cheyenne people had among them a prophet and teacher called *Sweet Medicine.*

Sweet Medicine was wise.

Sweet Medicine was good.

Sweet Medicine brought his people peace.

He himself did not want to be made their leader. "You should not have a leader more powerful than all the others," he said. He organized the tribe in such a way that there were forty-four chiefs who represented the tribe in all things and who were their leaders.

"A chief must not seek profit for himself," said Sweet Medicine. "He must help the people, live for the people, and, if need be, die for the people."

Warriors were greatly admired by the Cheyenne, but Sweet Medicine taught that when a man was chosen to be a chief, he must renounce his warrior ways and walk in the way of peace. A man could not be a soldier and a chief at the same time.

In case of war, the soldier societies did the fighting. They also carried out the punishment decided on by the Council of Chiefs for wrongdoing in the tribe. Always, however, the emphasis was on restitution, rehabilitation, and forgiveness.

How were the teachings of Sweet Medicine carried out in the lives of the Cheyenne? Did the teaching of Sweet Medicine make a difference in the way the people treated those who did wrong? Here is what happened.

One day in spring, at the beginning of the hunt, two young Cheyenne boys rode out to hunt buffalo by themselves, without waiting for the others. They wanted a head start. This was, of course, very selfish. It was also against the rules of communal hunting.

The Shield Society, whose duty it was to enforce the rules, saw the two and immediately swept down on them. As punishment they beat the boys and killed their horses. The boys' father came and lectured them about their selfish behavior.

Now the members of the Shield Society, who stood around them, saw that the boys were very ashamed of themselves. They had obviously learned their lesson. Two of the soldiers stepped forward and gave the boys horses. Two other soldiers gave them guns. The punishment of the culprits, their change of heart, and their rehabilitation took place within minutes. The matter was settled. This is the way the Cheyenne handled their own internal problems.

In 1825 something new happened in the life of the Cheyenne. The United States government sent an officer to ask them to come to Fort Teton to have a council meeting with them. The chiefs assembled, discussed this request, and decided to accept the invitation.

At the meeting the representatives of the United States government said, "Our people would like to travel through the country from east to west. May we have permission to build a road through your territory and use the water and the trees to help do this? We will only travel on the road and not trespass on any other land."

After the chiefs came home they held a tribal council about this.

"We have no ill will toward the white people," said one chief.

"Sweet Medicine taught that we should treat strangers as friends, make them welcome, and treat them as members of the tribe," said another chief.

53

"White people are loud and uncultured," said one of the chiefs slowly.

After a long silence another chief said, "True, but there is only a handful of them, and it can do little harm to let them cross our land."

"Yes, let them build the road," they finally all agreed. "By allowing them to do it, we will show our hospitality."

The Cheyenne kept their part of the treaty, but the white people did not. The handful of whites became a great stream moving from east to west. Instead of using only the road, they spread all across the country, and brought with them whiskey, sickness, and death.

The Cheyenne people became very angry. They wanted to fight back. What would the chiefs do now? Would they remember the teachings of Sweet Medicine? It became more and more difficult.

One year the Cheyenne were almost starving because they could not find any game. Suddenly they came upon six white hunters and beside them the carcasses of eighteen buffalo. They saw that the hunters had cut out only the tongues of the buffalo and were leaving the rest to rot!

The Cheyenne were furious. Slowly they surrounded the white hunters. The hunters knew that the Cheyenne were going to kill them.

But at that moment Chief Little Wolf, who was dedicated to the way of peace and to the teachings of Sweet Medicine, intervened. He smoked a pipe. He talked to the Cheyenne soldiers. Finally he turned to the hunters and in his powerful way he said, "Go!"

The hunters ran. They ran as fast as they could and never knew why their lives were spared!

But something even worse was about to happen. Chief Lean Bear was one of the chiefs who was greatly distressed over the turn of events. He wanted his people to live in peace with the white people. For this reason he and several other chiefs went to Washington in 1862 to speak with the president. Lean Bear was very happy when he came home. The president himself had spoken to them and assured them of the government's goodwill. Lean Bear brought back a peace medal the president had given him. He thought now they would all be able to live in peace.

Soon afterwards Lean Bear saw a column of white soldiers marching towards his camp. His people were frightened, but Lean Bear comforted them.

"Do not be afraid," he said. "The president himself has promised that no harm will come to us. See, I have hung his peace medal around my neck. And here are the papers he gave me."

Lean Bear and several of his men confidently rode out to meet the soldiers to tell them that this was a friendly camp. But the soldiers fired on Lean Bear before he could say anything. They killed him.

Now surely the Cheyenne would fight! Yes, in their fury, they started to fight the government soldiers. But another chief, Black Kettle, rode among them. He reasoned with them. He persuaded them once more to follow the teachings of Sweet Medicine and to keep the peace.

And so it was that long, long after Sweet Medicine had died, his teachings were still followed by the Cheyenne. This affected the lives of all the Cheyenne, and with them, the lives of all the white people. Sweet Medicine had truly been a great man.

Mr. No-Worry

Herr Ohnesorge

No-worry—that was actually his name. At least, that is the literal translation of the German name—Ohnesorge—of the man whose story I am about to tell.

Mr. No-worry was a theology student in Berlin. He had learned to put his trust in God, and since he had a happy nature his name was a very fitting one.

Before he became a pastor in a church, he had the opportunity of making a trip to the Holy Land. How happy he was to visit all the places where Jesus had walked! He was especially thrilled to be able to preach in Jerusalem.

Now southeast of Jerusalem there is an interesting mountain. From it you have an exceptional view of the whole country, so Mr. No-worry wanted very much to climb to its peak. His friends advised him not to do so without armed protection since bedouin robbers roved around in that region and made it very dangerous to travel alone.

Mr. No-worry just laughed. "No," he said, "I don't need any armed protection. The bedouins will see that I have nothing of any worth. They won't bother me."

Mr. No-worry had a great time. He climbed the mountain and finally stood on its very top. The view was breathtaking! Far below him he could see the Jordan winding its way like a green ribbon through the bare hills, and there in the distance was the Dead Sea! Mr. No-worry could not tear himself away from this beautiful spot.

Suddenly he sensed a movement behind one of the rocks. Yes, there it was again! A dark face with black piercing eyes was looking at him. And then another and another and another! In a matter of minutes a large group of bedouins was coming toward him. Mr. No-worry could not understand what they were saying, but he understood their menacing gestures only too well.

He took his watch and wallet out of his pocket and held them out to them with a friendly smile.

But that was not enough for them. Perhaps they were disappointed that there was not more to rob. Perhaps they just wanted to torment this stranger and make sport of him.

They took his coat. They took his vest. They pulled off his shirt and his trousers and made away with his shoes and stockings. With peals of malicious laughter the bedouins left Mr. No-worry standing there stark naked with only the black hat on his head!

What would the man who had no worries do now? How was he to get back to civilization with only a hat on his head? For a moment Mr. No-worry began to get worried. But only for a moment. Then his faith prevailed. He leaned against a huge rock and sang with a clear, strong voice the song which he had never before sung in such strange circumstances:

A mighty fortress is our God,
A bulwark never failing;
Our helper He amid the flood
Of mortal ills prevailing. . . .

On and on he sang until he came to the last verse:

Let goods and kindred go,
This mortal life also;
The body they may kill,
God's truth abideth still;
His kingdom is forever.

Then suddenly he saw the bedouins coming back. But this time there was an expression of awe on their faces. "A holy man, a holy man," they murmured. A holy man stands under the special protection of God and must not be hurt.

One by one they came and brought his things back: shirt and trousers, vest and coat, shoes and stockings, watch and wallet. Nothing was missing. Then they carefully guided him down the mountain to protect him from any other robbers.

With this unusual guard, Mr. No-worry reached Bethlehem. He had made it safely through bedouin territory! He did, indeed, have nothing to worry about.

A Bold New Plan

Richard Rush and Sir Charles Bagot   1817

The people in the United States went to church on Sunday and read in their Bibles the words of Jesus: "A new commandment I give to you, that you love one another; even as I have loved you" (John 13:34).

The people in Canada went to church on Sunday and read in their Bibles: "A new commandment I give to you, that you love one another; even as I have loved you."

But when the people in the United States went home from church they looked north and said, "Those Canadians! What are they up to now? Like as not, they are sending some more soldiers to the border. One of these nights they will come across to our side and kill us all."

The people in Canada went home from church and said, "Those Americans! Did you hear? They are getting a bigger and bigger army. They must be getting ready to attack us!"

Peace had been signed between Canada and the United States after the War of 1812, but people did not trust each other. They did not love each other. They liked to read Christ's words, but it did not occur to them to do as the words said.

"Let's train more soldiers," said the people in the United States.

"Let's send more armed forces to the border," cried the people in Canada.

"We don't have enough guns on that long boundary between us and those awful Canadians," said the people in the United States.

"Our forts need to be stronger," exclaimed the Canadians in fear. "The Americans can run right into our country."

"Send some more battleships into the Great Lakes," wrote the Americans to their congressmen. "That whole area is unprotected."

"What are those battleships doing in the Great Lakes?" asked the Canadians of their government. "We must arm our ships with bigger guns if our country is to be safe."

But there were some people in both countries who knew that a big army does not bring peace.

They were convinced that ships armed with guns do not create trust between people.

They felt that bigger and stronger forts do not keep a country safe.

Richard Rush of the State Department in Washington was one of those people who knew that armaments cannot solve political and economic problems. He went to the office of the British Ambassador, Sir Charles Bagot, who was in charge of Canadian affairs.

"Look," he said to Sir Bagot. "Our two countries are stationing more and more soldiers on either side of the border. This can only lead to more war."

"Yes," said Sir Bagot, "arming against each other will never bring peace. Only if we are friends will we feel safe along our border."

Richard Rush and Sir Charles Bagot went to work on a bold plan to protect their countries. It was new in the history of the world. In the treaty that they set up, they proposed the following:

1. Each country will let its soldiers go home.

2. All the battleships will be withdrawn from the Great Lakes.

3. All the forts along the U.S.A.-Canadian border will be destroyed.

Many people in both countries were horrified! "What? Leave the three-thousand-mile boundary unarmed and unprotected? This is ridiculous!"

But people who believed in love, not hate; in peace, not war; kept working diligently, and in

1817 the Rush-Bagot Agreement was signed.

After the people in the United States and the people in Canada had lived in peace along an unprotected border for a hundred years, they decided to celebrate.

In 1918 they built a gateway at Blaine, Washington. Half of the gateway stands in Canada and half in the United States. On the inside of the arch are inscribed these words: "Open for One Hundred Years—May These Doors Never Be Closed."

During the hundred years many problems arose between the United States and Canada, but always they were solved around a conference table instead of on a battlefield.

When people in the United States went to church and read the words of Jesus, "Love one another," they looked north and said, "Yes, on the other side of the border live our friends, the Canadians."

When the people in Canada went to church and read the words of Jesus, "Love one another," they said, "Yes, on the other side of the border live our friends, the Americans."

The bold new plan of Richard Rush and Charles Bagot had worked.

What Would Christ Have Done?

Claas Epp

The 1870s were troubled years for the Mennonites in Russia. They believed it was wrong to go to war because Christ taught his followers to love their enemies. When they had come to Russia from eastern Germany about a hundred years ago, they had been promised that their young men would never need to serve in the Armed Forces of Russia. But now that privilege was in danger of being withdrawn. They were threatened with the obligation of compulsory service. Because of this, about eighteen thousand Mennonites emigrated to the United States and Canada.

There was a small group of people, however, who believed that Christ would return very shortly. One of their leaders, Claas Epp, preached eloquently that the Mennonites must go east to Turkestan to escape military service and to meet the Lord when he returned. About six hundred Mennonites believed Claas Epp and migrated to Turkestan to wait for the Lord's coming. When Christ did not return as Claas Epp prophesied, that was a terrible blow to all of them. But there was something else that greatly disturbed their faith, and that is what this story is all about.

After unbelievable hardships and much suffering, a smaller group, including Claas Epp, settled on a hill among Turkeman neighbors. The Turkemans seemed friendly enough during the daytime, but in reality were very hostile. They were jealous of the Mennonites and resented the small settlement in their midst.

One morning one Mennonite family found one of their horses had been stolen during the night. The man went over to the Turkemans living nearby and accused them of stealing it.

"We did not steal it," they said angrily. "And

we certainly do not appreciate being blamed for something another clan has done."

After that many horses were stolen from the people on the hill. At first the thieves came stealthily, but when they found out that the Mennonites did not oppose them, they became more and more brazen.

They took the horses out of the barns, locked or unlocked, day or night. Some even rode the stolen horses up to the homes of the Mennonites, dismounted, walked into the house, took clothing and other things, and rode away.

Since the Mennonites believed that they should not resist evil with force, the Turkemans became bolder and bolder and ever more violent. Soon they forced their way into the homes. Screaming, they would shoot into a window, break down the door, and drive the people out. After that they vandalized the home; they cut up the bedding, destroyed clocks and other useful articles, and broke tables and chairs to make a fire.

Finally it got too much for some of the people. Two Mennonites tried to stop the Turkemans and were stabbed with sabers. Hearing the commotion, the neighbors came running. The Mennonites beat the robbers' horses with sticks until the horses ran away, carrying the riders with them.

Now the young men of the Mennonite settlement wanted to fight back. They demanded weapons to defend themselves!

"The reason why the Turkemans have become so bold," said one young man bitterly, is because they know that Christianity teaches us that if anyone takes away our coat, we are to let him have our cloak also. So why should they not demand our property?"

Another man added, "If the Turkemans are not shown the error of their ways, they will destroy our whole colony. We must be able to drive them away."

"Jesus cannot have meant that we must let them get away with everything," said another. "It doesn't make sense."

The leaders of the community were very uneasy. What should they do? Had they moved all the way to Asia because they did not believe in going to war, only to give up their nonresistance at the first test in living with non-Christian neighbors?

After much discussion, they finally gave permission to the young men to arm themselves with canes, clubs, and sticks, in order to defend the settlement. At least they would not shoot anyone.

When the Turkemans attacked a house that night, seven young men with their makeshift weapons blocked the way.

"Move!" yelled the robbers.

"No, we will not move!" replied the night watchmen stoutly. They stood their ground, but all seven were wounded.

One young Mennonite, hiding on a roof, yelled at a Turkeman. The Turkeman wheeled around, fired his rifle, and hit the young man with buckshot.

Another group of guards galloped off in another direction, hoping to draw the robbers after them away from the Mennonite homes, but this did not work either. Another large band of Turkemans stopped them and stole all their horses! The whole thing was a failure.

Then something happened that topped all other Turkeman misdeeds and called for definite action. One day some of the Turkemans jokingly offered to buy Heinrich Abrahm's pretty young wife, Elizabeth. The next night a band of Turkemans crept into the Abrahm's home to steal Elizabeth. Elizabeth woke up suddenly when she heard a strange noise. Her husband jumped out of bed immediately and rushed to the door to frighten the robbers away. But the Turkemans shot him on the spot and repeatedly stabbed his body. Meanwhile, his wife climbed out of the bedroom window and ran to the neighbors across the street, where she hid.

When the men of the village arrived on the scene, the robbers were gone and their neighbor Abrahms was dead. They immediately formed a search party to track down the murderers. Riding around the hill, they came upon the bandits dividing the goods they had stolen from the Abrahms' home.

A Mennonite man, Peter Unruh, called, "You thieves and murderers! What are you doing?"

Immediately the bandits surrounded him and his companions. They ordered Unruh to kneel down. "Pray to your God," they shouted, "for we are going to shoot you for calling us thieves and murderers!"

"Why did you mercilessly kill that young man?" asked Unruh.

"Because he did not want to let us have what we wanted," replied one of the Turkemans.

With that they raised their guns.

But before they could shoot, Johann Drake, a young Mennonite, jumped into the circle, raised Peter Unruh to his feet and put his arms around him.

"Brother, I will die for you," he said. Then he looked at the Turkemans and said, "Take me in place of this man. I am alone, and he has a wife and small children."

This surprised the Turkemans. "No," said one of them. "This we cannot do, because not only does our religion forbid it, but it is also against our conscience. Go away and let us quickly kill this man who called us thieves and robbers."

Drake did not move. He kept his arms around Unruh. The bandits began murmuring among themselves. Finally they lowered their guns and said, "We grant you both your freedom and your lives." Then they mounted their horses and rode away.

When local Turkeman authorities were notified about the murder, they merely suggested that the Mennonites should build their houses closer together, build walls around them, and buy guns for protection! So now the Mennonites really had to face it: did nonresistance work in real-life situations or did it not?

The settlers debated it over and over again.

"Let us hire several Cossack watchmen to protect the settlement," said one voice.

"Never!" retorted several others. "How is that different than shooting someone ourselves? Don't we believe in nonresistance anymore?"

Silence.

"We should never have come here," said a voice helplessly.

"We should have migrated to America," said another. "I just received a letter from my brother, and he says nobody is molesting them there!"

"Ha!" said a young voice sharply. "And why not? Because hired government policemen are protecting the settlements, that's why!"

"So why shouldn't we also hire our policemen?" called a chorus of voices.

"If we do that, it is the same as saying that Christ's commandment to love our enemies is impractical and impossible," said a voice quietly but distinctly.

Silence.

Finally a voice which had never spoken before said, "We all know we have a serious problem. It strikes at the very heart of our belief and the reason for our coming here. We are followers of Christ, and so I have been thinking of what Christ would have done had he come here when he was on earth."

Everyone listened in expectation.

"First of all, I think he would have walked among the Turkemans and sat with them. He would have been their friend, and we were not."

Nobody said anything.

"Furthermore, Christ would have shared what he had with the Turkemans," the voice went on. "We knew of their extreme poverty, but we never thought of sharing voluntarily what little we had."

Nobody said anything.

"Christ would have told them of the love of our Father. We had our services several times each Sunday and also during the week, but we never included our neighbors."

Still no one spoke.

"And then Christ died for all of us, because he loves us. Do we love our Turkeman neighbors? Are we willing to die for them even as our brother Johann Drake was ready to die for one of us? It seems to me we have left an important part out of our nonresistance, and without that, nonresistance becomes a farce. The love of Christ is what makes it real."

The voice stopped speaking, and it was as if a sigh went through the congregation.

After a long time, another voice said, "I see that we have treated our nonresistance as something separate from the rest of Christ's teachings. We have sinned. We are an imperfect people, even when forgiven."

"We shall always be imperfect," responded another voice. "But even if we do not demonstrate nonresistance perfectly, we must continue to live by that rule as best we can."

"The best we can do right now is to hire armed people to protect us," said a voice impatiently. "In the meantime we can work on the other aspects of nonresistance. Who would vote for that?"

Although there were people who were deeply troubled, the majority agreed with the suggestion, and so two Cossack nightwatchmen were hired. They were excellent marksmen with rifles, and everyone knew it. A few nights after they began their work, several Turkemans tried to raid a Mennonite walled compound. The Cossacks simply fired over their heads, and they retreated. From then on there were very few robberies and assaults.

How do you feel about this story? Did the Mennonites do the right thing? What would *you* have done?

Why Are You Praying for Me?

Elizabeth Fry   1780-1845

Elizabeth Fry was horrified at the conditions of the prisons in England in her day. She worked untiringly to bring about reforms. "Prisoners need help rather than punishment in order to become good citizens," she insisted.

During her work in Bristol, she stayed in an inn. How glad she was to leave the cold, dark, and drafty prison after a day's work and come to a place where it was warm! She ran up the steps to her room and opened the door.

Elizabeth Fry stopped short. Something was wrong, but what was it? Her eyes fastened on the dresser drawer. Surely she had not left it open like that! And the shawl that she had not worn at all for several days was flung over a chair! Disturbed, she looked down and saw a candle from the nightstand lying on the floor. And under her bed—! Elizabeth's heart almost stopped. Just below the edge of the patchwork quilt, she saw the sole of a man's boot. There was a man under her bed!

"Now, Elizabeth, don't panic!" she told herself. What should she do? To give herself time to think, she put the shawl back into the drawer and closed it. Then she slowly picked up the candle. By this time she had reached a decision.

She knelt down beside the boot. She could hear the man breathing hard. He was probably terrified at being caught.

"Dear Lord," prayed Elizabeth Fry, "please forgive this man for what he has done. May your goodness enter his heart and help him to improve his ways." Her voice was soft and kind.

The boot stirred.

"Dear Lord," continued Elizabeth, "this man is confused and needs your guidance so that he will steal no more."

The man crawled out from under the bed. He was very thin and dirty.

"Why are you praying for me?" he demanded gruffly. "Why don't you call the innkeeper and get it over with?"

"The Lord is the only one I'll call. Thee must have had a very special reason for coming into my room," said Elizabeth as she rose from her knees.

The man looked down.

"Can't thee tell me what it is?" asked Elizabeth gently.

The man was silent. Elizabeth waited.

"I'm hungry, ma'am," he blurted out at last. "I've been hungry for days. I've been stealing scraps of food, but that didn't fill the empty hole here in my stomach. I needed money for real food. And I've been so cold, I was looking for a coat."

"I'm glad thee came to my room," said Elizabeth Fry. "I think I can help thee."

The man looked at her as if she could not be real.

Elizabeth pulled out a heavy sweater of her husband's and gave it to the man.

"Now come downstairs with me and I'll ask the innkeeper to give thee a real dinner."

The man's eyes suddenly darted toward the window with a wild look. "And then you will have me put into prison?" he demanded.

"No," said Elizabeth, "I'm too well acquainted with prisons—I would not ever send anyone there."

"You mean you've been in prison, ma'am?" asked the man in astonishment.

"Yes, I've been in many, many prisons," answered Elizabeth Fry with a chuckle.

"So have I, but that's nothing to laugh about," glowered the man. "Whatever could you have done to get thrown into one of those holes?"

"I'll tell thee about it while thee eats dinner," answered Elizabeth, and she led the man downstairs to the big hall in the inn.

Companionably Elizabeth Fry and the burglar sat down to eat. Elizabeth told him about her work in the prisons, and the man told her about his unhappy and desperate life. Together they planned how he could get out of his life of crime and find work.

The man had entered the inn as a burglar. He left it with the lightest heart he had ever known. At last he had the courage to start over again.

64

Father, Forgive Them

Seth Loflin   Between 1861 and 1865

The Civil War was raging in the United States. Brother fought against brother. Each was ready to die for that which he believed to be right. Many thought it was wrong to own slaves and quoted the Bible to prove it. Others said it was right to own slaves and also quoted the Bible to prove it. In the meantime blood flowed, and hatred in the country grew.

Seth Loflin did not believe killing each other was the way to settle the problem. He took no sides. He was sure Christ had shown a better way than war to bring about good.

When Seth was called up for military service, he refused to shoulder a gun and explained that it was against his conscience to do so. But the army was in no mood to put up with such nonsense. The officers considered themselves Christians, but this they could not understand. Seth Loflin was promptly thrown into prison. Over and over again he was commanded to take up arms and to fight, but always he refused.

Finally he faced a court-martial.

"Seth Loflin," began the presiding officer, "this court is unanimous in finding you guilty of the gravest insubordination. We do not believe that it is wrong for a Christian man to bear arms."

There was a murmur of approval from the soldiers present.

"With your conscience we are not concerned," the officer continued. "With your military service we are, and since you continue to defy all lawfully constituted authority, the court sentences you to be suspended by your thumbs for one hour. If, after this punishment, you wish to take your place with your regiment, you may."

Seth Loflin gave no sign of his inward feelings. Silently he followed his guard who led him to his torture. After the dreadful hour was over, Seth was left to crawl back to his tent. His body was almost worn out by a succession of punishments. He lay on his bed, with eyes closed, and prayed.

Some of the soldiers felt sorry for him. "Come, Loflin," they begged, "make the best of a bad job and shoulder a rifle. It is the only way out."

Seth shook his head. "Thank you for your kindness, fellows," he said, "but I can't disobey Christ, my Supreme Commander."

The next day Seth was again ordered to pick up his gun and march with his regiment. Again he refused.

Once more he faced the court. "I cannot kill another human being," he said. "Christ taught us to love our enemies. I must obey him rather than you."

There was no question about it this time. Seth Loflin was sentenced to die.

"This man will be shot in the presence of all ranks in camp," said the presiding officer. "We are going to make an example of him. The discipline of the army must be preserved."

"I would rather be killed than kill another," said Seth Loflin.

At the appointed hour on the appointed day, company after company of men marched into the parade ground. They all knew what they were about to see.

Eddies of dust swirled about marching feet as line after line of soldiers marched, halted, and turned, until three sides of a square were completed.

As the drums started beating, officers of high rank took their places. The firing squad came in and took its position. They loaded their rifles.

Last of all, a guard brought in the prisoner.

A silence as still as death hung over the awful

scene. Seth's hands were tied and his eyes were bandaged. The guard led him to the wall which formed the fourth side of the square and turned him about to face the firing squad.

"May I have a moment or two to pray, sir?" asked Seth.

The officer in charge of the execution hesitated a moment. The request was so unusual that he did not know what he should do. But then he stepped aside so that the prisoner could be by himself.

After a few minutes' silence, Seth's clear voice, speaking without a tremor, could be heard by everyone present: "Father, forgive them, for they know not what they do!"

In a moment the whole atmosphere was tense with emotion. The officer in charge sensed that he should never have granted the prisoner's request.

"Firing party, ready!" he shouted. The men stiffened to attention.

"Prepare to fire!" Six rifles came up to six shoulders, but very haltingly.

The officer saw what was the matter, and with an oath called, "Fire!"

The rifles wobbled and finally pointed downward. Nobody fired.

White with fury, the officer demanded, "What do you think you are doing?"

"Can't shoot him, sir," said one. The others murmured agreement. There was a wave of approval from the soldiers who made up the square.

Other officers quickly took over and marched Seth Loflin away.

Although the death sentence was later canceled, Loflin died in the hospital because of the suffering he had endured. He was ready to meet his Supreme Commander. The order was "Love your enemy," and that he had obeyed.

I Want Revenge

Captain Conolly's Sister

Dr. Pennell stepped out of the door of the hospital. He had seen a group of men coming down the hill with a stretcher.

"Whom are you bringing?" he asked the men as they lowered the stretcher in front of him.

The men shrugged their shoulders. "We don't know. We found the man lying by the side of the road. He is seriously wounded. Do you have room for him, Sahib? We want to leave him here and continue on our way."

The doctor bent over the man on the stretcher. He could tell that the patient was an Afghan, a member of the Patau tribe which was always at war with the surrounding population.

"Bring him in," said the doctor. "For him we have a bed."

After the patient was settled, Dr. Pennell came to examine him.

"Sahib," moaned the patient, trying to tear the bandage off his eyes, "give me back my sight! Then I can go and find the man that did this to me. I want revenge! I want to kill him. After that I don't care whether I am blind the rest of my life!"

Dr. Pennell was well acquainted with the custom of revenge. "My friend," he answered the man in his own language, "you are in a Christian hospital. Our Lord Jesus Christ, who commanded me to build this house, wants us to learn to forgive our enemies."

The doctor sat down beside the man and told him about the Son of God who came into this world to show us the way of love and to die for us.

"Sahib," the man interrupted the doctor, "those are nice words, but they mean nothing to me. I just want revenge! Revenge! My enemy took my eyes. He will have to pay for it with his life. There is nothing more powerful than revenge!"

The doctor rose from his chair. "I have to go now since many other patients are waiting for me, but tonight I shall come back and tell you a story. It is about a person who took revenge. It happened in this area."

The man heard the steps of the doctor walking away from him; then he was alone again in his darkness. He couldn't help thinking about what the doctor had said. He waited for evening to come.

Finally the doctor came back, sat down beside his bed, and started to tell the story.

"Many years ago," he said, "the British government sent Captain Conolly as an envoy to Afghanistan. He never arrived in the capital, however. On a lonely stretch of the road, he was seized by a tribe of that country. They took away his baggage, bound him, accused him of espionage, and threw him into prison. He had no idea what would happen to him.

"Fortunately, another man, Captain Stoddard, who some time before had also been seized without reason and imprisoned, was in the same jail. The two men were very glad that they could at least be together.

"Weeks and months went by in terrible monotony. The guards mistreated them. The food was bad and very scarce. The only light they had in their cell came from a hole near the ceiling.

"In their misery the two men had only one comfort. That was a little prayer book that the guards had allowed Captain Conolly to keep. He had received it as a farewell gift from his sister when he left for India. The prayer book showed them the ground of their being and pointed to the highest to which their souls could aspire. The prayers and the songs comforted them; they felt the presence of the Lord Jesus Christ in their cell.

"The prayer book did something else. The two men were able to persuade the guards to give them a pen and something like ink to write with. Now they filled the margins of the little book with reports of their experiences as prisoners. They also wrote how they felt about those experiences and what effect they had on their souls. The prayer book became a diary of their prison life.

"A whole year passed by. The last entry in the prayer book was by someone else. It said that the two men had been brought out of prison, publicly flogged, and then had been forced to dig two graves.

"They were never seen again. No one except the tribe in Afghanistan knew about their execution. In vain their families, their friends, and the government in England waited for some news of them. Twenty-one years went by.

"Then it so happened that one day a Russian officer was sauntering along a street in Buchara, a city in central Asia. He stopped in a second-hand shop. Among the odds and ends he discovered an English prayer book with all kinds of entries in the margins which he could not decipher. He saw a name and address on the flyleaf, however. 'Perhaps this little book is important to someone,' he thought to himself,

and sent it to England.

"That is how Captain Conolly's sister received the prayer book which she had given to her brother twenty-one years before!

"With great anguish she read the account of the prison experiences of her brother and his friend and was greatly moved by their thoughts during the days before their execution.

"What should she do? The terrible injustice done to her brother called for revenge. For Christian revenge! She was not wealthy, but she sent all the money that she could to Dr. Pennell's hospital with these instructions: 'Please keep a bed free in your hospital at all times for a sick or wounded Afghan, and use the money to take care of him until he regains his health. I am doing this in memory of my brother who suffered so much at the hands of Afghans and who died in their country.'"

There was complete silence at the bed of the wounded Afghan when Dr. Pennell had finished his story. The doctor put his hand on the shoulder of the blind man. "My friend," he said, "you are now lying in that bed. That you are being taken care of is a revenge for the death of Captain Conolly."

For the first time in his life, the man who so passionately desired revenge and who had so curtly rejected the message of Christ sensed a power that is stronger than hate. It is the power of love.

Serves Him Right!

E. G. Kaufman

When Ed Kaufman was a boy, he went to a little country school in Kansas. On the playground and in the classroom there were children whose parents had originally come from Switzerland; there were children whose parents had come from Russia; there were children whose parents and grandparents and great-grandparents had always lived in the United States.

Sometimes all these children got along very well, but sometimes they didn't. The native Kansans teased the Swiss, the Swiss teased the Low Germans from Russia, and the Low Germans teased both the Kansans and the Swiss. Mostly it was all in fun, but now and then feelings were really hurt.

Now there was a boy called Peter who was always jumping on Ed. He wrestled Ed down whenever he could, and since he was bigger and stronger, Ed didn't have a chance. When they were on the playground, Pete took advantage of Ed every time.

One day in the winter the wind was blowing up an honest-to-goodness blizzard, and it was very cold. Ed saw Pete coming into the school-house slapping his cold hands and rubbing his cheeks. With his usual determination Pete elbowed his way close to the potbellied stove to warm himself.

The stove was red-hot. First Pete held his hands towards it. When they were a little warmer and his face was hot, he turned around and backed close to the stove to warm his behind. His clothes were wet with snow.

Ed was watching him closely. Suddenly it seemed to Ed that there was a wisp of smoke coming from roughly the area where the seat of Pete's pants would be.

"Ha!" thought Ed. "Serves him right!"

Fascinated, Ed saw the wisp of smoke get larger. How long would it take to burn through the seat of Pete's pants, and how would Pete look then? Ed chuckled inwardly. He knew he should warn Pete, but he sure didn't want to. Pete had been so mean to him. He was his enemy. Enemy?

But people of peace should love their enemies and be good to them, popped into Ed's mind. It bothered him, but it was so much fun watching that smoke and seeing Pete standing there so unconcerned that he put if off just a little bit longer.

Suddenly Pete smelled the smoke. "Hey, my pants are burning!" he yelled. Frantically he tried to put out the flames.

At this point Ed graciously rushed to the rescue. He was afraid more of Pete would burn than just the seat of his pants! Together the two enemies extinguished the smoldering cloth.

"Thanks—Pal!" said Pete.

Years later the two boys, now grown-up men, met again.

"Do you remember when the seat of your pants burned?" asked Ed.

"I sure do," answered Pete. "And I also remember how you helped me!"

Then they both laughed.

69

Wise as Solomon
1913

Peter Janzen had just been baptized. He was twenty years old, and he wondered what kind of work the Lord would have for him. He did not have long to wait. The first assignment God gave him was a most interesting one.

Peter's father, who was a minister, had to go on a longer trip, and so his wife accompanied him. Peter was left alone to mind the farm. The Janzens lived in a Mennonite village in Russia.

One day Peter saw a carriage drawn by brown horses come up the driveway. It stopped in front of their door. In the carriage sat a man and his wife. The woman, a pert little thing with a white kerchief tied at the back of her head, jumped down from the carriage.

When Peter came out, she said, "Good morning!"

"Good morning," Peter responded.

"Is your father at home?" she asked.

"No," said Peter. "He is on a trip."

"When will he be back?"

"I don't know," said Peter. "Probably next week sometime."

"Thank you," said the woman. She got back into the carriage and, together with her husband, drove away again.

Pretty soon a carriage drawn by black horses came up the driveway. In it again sat a man and his wife. When the carriage stopped, the woman, also with a white kerchief on her head, jumped down and came to the door.

"Good morning," she said.

"Good morning," Peter responded.

"Is your father at home?" asked this woman also.

"No," said Peter. "He is on a trip."

"When will he be back?" asked the woman.

"I don't know," said Peter. "Probably next week sometime."

"Thank you," said the woman. She got back into the carriage and, together with her husband, drove off.

On Monday of the next week, Peter suddenly saw Carriage No. 1 with the brown horses come up the driveway again. As before, the pert little woman with the white kerchief on her head jumped off and came to the door.

"Good morning!" she said.

"Good morning!" Peter responded.

"Is your father at home now?" she asked.

"No, he isn't back yet," answered Peter.

"When will he come?" she asked.

"I don't know," said Peter. "Maybe on Wednesday."

"Thank you," said the woman. She got into the carriage and, together with her husband, drove off again.

Peter looked out of the window. Sure enough, it did not take too long before Carriage No. 2 with the black horses came up the driveway. As before, the woman jumped off the carriage and came to the door.

"Good morning!" she said.

"Good morning!" Peter responded.

"Is your father at home now?" she asked, even as the woman in Carriage No. 1 had done.

"No," replied Peter, "he isn't back yet."

"When will he come?" she asked.

"I don't know," said Peter. "Maybe on Wednesday."

"Thank you," said the woman. She got back into the carriage and, together with her husband, drove off.

When Wednesday came, Peter's parents had still not come home.

But Carriage No. 1 soon turned into their

driveway again. The pert little woman in the white kerchief jumped off the carriage and came to the door.

"Has your father come home?" she asked.

"No," said Peter. "He isn't back yet."

"Then I will tell *you* my problem," she said.

"Oh, no!" exclaimed Peter. "I wouldn't do that if I were you. I am very young and don't know much."

"But you are a minister's son. You will know what to do."

Not knowing how to turn them away, Peter asked the couple into the living room where his father usually counseled with the members of his congregation.

"This spring," began the woman, "one of our neighbor's hens came into our yard and laid twelve eggs under the hedge. As you know, eggs in our village always belong to the yard where they are found. In due time the hen sat on the eggs and hatched twelve chicks—on our side of the fence, mind you! My neighbor, though, says those chicks belong to her! What do *you* say?" The little woman stemmed her arms in her sides defiantly. "Whose chicks are they?"

"Hmm," said Peter. "Hmmmm!" His mind went into high gear and his eyes began to twinkle.

"I would suggest," he said very seriously, "that you kill the hen, cook chicken noodle soup out of it, and ask your neighbors for supper. As for the chicks—you can divide them evenly. Give six to your neighbor and keep six."

"Come, Mother," said the woman's husband. "The matter is settled. We shall go home now."

With that, the man and his wife climbed back into their carriage and drove away.

A little later, as on the previous days, Carriage No. 2 came up the driveway. The woman jumped off the carriage and came to the door.

"Has your father come home?" she asked.

"No," said Peter. "He isn't back yet."

"Then I will tell *you* my problem," said this woman also.

"Oh, no, no!" exclaimed Peter. "I wouldn't do that if I were you. I am very young and don't know much."

"But you are a minister's son and will know what to do," said the woman.

Peter asked the couple into the living room. They all sat down.

"This spring," began the woman, "one of my hens happened to stray into the neighbor's yard. She laid twelve eggs there and later hatched them. Now my neighbor says the twelve chicks are hers. I say they are mine." The woman's eyes were flashing dangerously. "Tell me, whose chicks are they?"

"Well," said Peter, "a little while ago your neighbor was here and told me of this problem with the chicks. I suggested to her that she kill the hen, cook chicken noodle soup, and ask you for supper so you could eat it together. Then you could divide the chicks evenly. She could have six and you could have six. Apparently that is what they are going to do."

"Good!" said the woman's husband. "Come, Mother, the matter is settled. Let us go home."

With that the man and his wife got into the carriage and drove away.

Peter's parents came home the next day. Some time later Peter saw his mother looking at him with a peculiar expression on her face. Her lips were twitching!

"Why are you looking at me that way?" asked Peter. "What have I done now?"

"Oh, nothing," said his mother laughing. "But do you know what the people in the village are saying about you?"

"No," said Peter.

"They say you are as wise as Solomon!"

Could He Ever Be the Same Again?

Elizabeth Caraman

It was the year 1917. The place was an Armenian hospital in Mezre. Day after day, Elizabeth Caraman, a nurse in that hospital, cleansed and bound up the wounds of Turkish soldiers who had been wounded on the battlefields. Often when the soldiers came to her, hastily applied bandages were dried on to a gaping wound. It was extremely painful to remove them.

One day Elizabeth was working on a specially bad wound. To help the young soldier think about something besides the pain, she told him a little about her own history.

"My father and I were deported from our home by the Turks," she said bitterly, "and my father was thrown into prison. In 1915 they took him out of his cell, rolled him in a carpet and hoisted him up on a donkey. Together with other Armenian men they sent him away to die."

At this moment, Elizabeth, for some reason, looked up. To her surprise the young soldier was staring at her with a look of horror in his black eyes.

"What is the matter?" Elizabeth asked.

"I killed your father," he said in a low voice.

Elizabeth could only gasp. She had never heard how her father had died. With a superhuman effort, she went on cleansing the wound.

"I rolled him off the donkey onto the ground," the soldier continued. "With one jab of the bayonet I killed him. I have never been able to forget it. The whole business of killing has sickened me."

Elizabeth felt a wave of hatred and sorrow sweep over her. Here was the murderer of her father. In some strange way, the enemy had fallen into her hands. She had the power to destroy him.

At this moment Elizabeth thought of her mother. What would she have done? Her mother loved Christ and tried to follow him. She would have tried to help this young man. The power and light of her mother's life reached out to Elizabeth.

Gently Elizabeth turned to the soldier lying in front of her. "Christ says we must forgive our enemies. For his sake, I forgive you," she said.

The soldier stared at her in amazement. He could not say anything. Every day, when Elizabeth came to his bed to dress his wound, she saw him looking at her with awe and wonder in his eyes.

Finally, one day, he said to Elizabeth, "Your Christ must be very great! His teachings really live in your heart, for I see them in your life."

How glad Elizabeth was that God had given her the power to forgive her enemy! It had cleansed all bitterness from her soul. Now she was free to love and live again.

In a Prison

Mathilda Wrede   1864-1928

Very early in life Mathilda Wrede had a vision. Three times God showed her the picture of a convict who raised his handcuffed hands toward her in silent agony.

The next morning when Mathilda got up and walked out into the garden surrounding the palace where she lived, she saw to her amazement the identical man at work. He was from the prison at Vasa where her father was governor.

Mathilda felt she had to talk to him. Timidly she walked over to the man. What should she say? It was very embarrassing, but she managed to say something about the love of God. She didn't know whether the man heard her or not, but finally he raised his head, looked straight at her, and said, "It is too bad that you don't come down there into our prison to talk to all of us."

That was Mathilda Wrede's call. For many, many years she worked with the prisoners in Finland. They knew her well. She who loved the great outdoors and the freedom of sun and wind, now walked into the awful stench of the dark, dank cells of the prison, heard the terrible clatter of chains, and saw the angry faces of evil, tormented men. Wherever she went, she brought compassion and understanding. The prisoners knew Mathilda Wrede cared about them.

One day Mathilda was going to visit a dangerous criminal. She did not know it, but the man had vowed to murder the next person who would enter his cell. When Mathilda entered, the man looked at her like a beast of prey ready to pounce on its victim.

"Ha, ha, ha," he laughed hoarsely. "What a fine visitor I have today! Won't you sit down, Madam?"

Mathilda calmly sat down on the old bench against the wall.

"Now, then," continued the man mockingly, "why have you come?"

"I have come to help you in any way I can," said Mathilda Wrede warmly. "Do you have any family members to whom you would like to send greetings or to whom you would like me to write?"

"That's a fine excuse!" scoffed the man. "I know why you have really come. You want to preach at me, that's why!"

He watched her with leering eyes. What would she say to that?

"No," said Mathilda emphatically. "I will not talk to you about God now. Some other day, when you really want to know about him, I will be most happy to do so, but certainly not now."

The man was rather surprised at his visitor's poise and serenity. Was she really not afraid of him? He sat down beside her on the bench in such a way that he blocked the door, her only way of escape.

But Mathilda thought only of this poor giant of a man. How terrible it must be for him, accustomed to the freedom of the forest, to be caged up in this narrow cell! Listening to the voice of God had taught Mathilda Wrede to listen to the unexpressed anguish of the human heart. The man's need became her need.

Somehow the criminal sensed this. How could he kill this woman? But he had sworn that he would kill the next person who would enter his cell! Of course he had never dreamed that it would be a woman. His frustration became intolerable.

"I vowed I would murder the next person who would enter my cell," he finally panted. "Get out of here fast, before I do it!"

Mathilda looked at him with her great, dark eyes. "But if I go, then you will murder the next person who comes?"

"Yes. My mind is made up."

"Then I will stay," said Mathilda. She folded her hands and waited.

God alone knows what went on in the hearts of these two people. There was silence. Only the chains that fettered the man to the wall rattled, and now and then the groans of a man in torment could be heard. Finally he uttered a wild shriek.

What would he do?

The huge man threw himself on the ground in front of Mathilda and wept like a child.

Mathilda's life was saved. But the story is not over. A ray of heavenly light had entered the heart of the criminal that day. Many and many a time Mathilda revisited him, and the time did come indeed when he wanted to know more about God. Mathilda's patience bore fruit.

Won't You Have Lunch with Me?

Mathilda Wrede   1864-1928

Mathilda Wrede, the friend of the prisoners in Finland, also did much to help needy people when the Russian Revolution of 1917 spread to her country. Those were hard times. There was violence and brutality. People lined up into opposing camps. They hated each other. Slowly famine spread across the land. Those who were not killed by the sword often died of hunger or disease.

Mathilda Wrede refused to take sides. She believed in the healing power of God's love. No matter which side people were on, Mathilda helped them if she could possibly do so.

One morning Mathilda's assistant slipped into her room white as a sheet. "There are several revolutionaries in the hall and many more outside," she whispered. "What shall we do?"

"Do?" repeated Mathilda surprised. "Why, ask them in to see me, of course."

The next moment they came in.

"Good morning, boys!" said Mathilda Wrede in her clear, friendly voice. "What do you want?"

"Money!" they growled.

"I have some in the house, but it has been given for the old and the sick," replied Mathilda firmly.

"That may be," they said threateningly, "but we are hungry and we want money."

"Why, of course," replied Mathilda, "you must be hungry! Won't you share my lunch with me? I was just going to start eating."

With that, Mathilda lifted the cover from the tray on her desk. There on a plate the intruders saw, in this year of famine, a little bit of boiled cabbage and a slice of bread!

The men stared at the plate. They looked at each other.

"It is Miss Wrede," said one of them in a hoarse whisper.

Silently the men filed out of the room. They made no more demands.

The Little Teacher

Catherine Hine

Catherine Hine was a soldier of the Salvation Army in London around the turn of the century. Faithfully she gathered the Chinese people who lived around the docks to tell them the good news of Jesus Christ. The work was difficult. But gradually many Chinese learned to love "the little teacher," as they called her. They sensed that what she had to tell them was of utmost importance to their lives.

Those who were ready for it formed a group for more intensive Bible study. To these Catherine also showed the flag of the Salvation Army. She hung it on the wall and explained its meaning.

"The red of the flag stands for the blood of Christ, which was shed for all people," she said. "The narrow blue band signifies the people—brave and true—that follow Jesus Christ, and the yellow star is a symbol of the fire of the Holy Spirit. The Spirit's fruits are love, joy, and peace" (Gal. 5:22).

When the participants left the Bible study session, Catherine Hine said, "*Ping an*—Peace be to you!"

One day a man by the name of Sung, who had been faithfully attending the Bible studies, came to Catherine to say good-bye to her.

"I have decided to return to China," he said. "I am tired of the life at sea and want to go back to the village where I grew up."

As he was leaving, the little teacher gave him a small replica of the Salvation Army flag. "*Yi lu king*," she said—"A peace assignment for you."

Sung returned to his village in China. Nothing had changed there. The people were doing the same tasks they had always done, and they were still worshiping the spirits of their ancestors. Sung told them about the little teacher and her

work and message. The people were glad that someone had been so kind to him, but the message of Jesus Christ, which he proclaimed to them over and over again, they rejected. They could not understand how Sung could believe what to them was utter nonsense. Sung remembered how patient the little teacher had been with all of them in London. He tried to be patient also.

At this time the Boxer Rebellion broke out in China and soon after developed into a civil war. Two opposing Chinese armies fought each other unto death.

One day the people in the village where Sung lived heard the news that an enemy army was approaching, burning and destroying everything in its path. The people were terror-stricken. What should they do? No one knew an answer. Even the priests could not help.

In desperation they turned to Sung. "Would your God be able to save us?" they asked.

Sung thought hard. In London, when the little teacher spoke, it had been easy to believe that with God all things are possible and that God would protect him. But now, with the army whom no one could withstand marching toward his little village? Sung was afraid. But at the same time he knew that the Word of God was true in both good and difficult times. He, as a good soldier of Jesus Christ, must now try to make peace, even if it meant facing danger and death.

Suddenly Sung remembered the little flag. He had never used it. But the little teacher had given it to him for a purpose. "A peace assignment for you," she had said. Should he go to meet the enemy with the little flag? The flag helped him to remember the little teacher and the Lord Jesus Christ. What he would do with the flag, he did not know, but he decided to go. Since he was the only soldier of Jesus Christ in the village, it made sense to him that he must go alone. God would help him.

The villagers were aghast when he told them of his plan. Why was he willing to do such a thing? How could he be so calm about his dreadful mission?

Sung, with the flag in his hand, walked toward the enemy camp. The guards treated him roughly, but consented to take him to the general. Sung had no idea what he could possibly do to save the village, but inwardly he was calm. "Your heavenly Father knows what you need," he said to himself.

He was taken into a large tent. There he stood before the general.

To Sung's bewilderment, the general took no notice of him. He just stared at the little flag in Sung's hand.

"It is the flag of the little teacher," the general said at last. He turned to Sung. "I used to visit her Bible classes in London too. Tell me, is she still alive? And is she still helping us Chinese?"

While Sung told the general everything he knew about Catherine Hine, there was a faraway look in the general's eyes. He thought he was done with that part of his life, but now, seeing the flag in the hand of Sung, it all rose up in him again. He had been very close to becoming a Christian and dedicating his life to the building of God's kingdom, but he had never taken that step.

After Sung finished his story about Catherine, there was complete silence in the tent. Both Sung and the general were suddenly aware again of the present situation. What would the general do?

It did not take him long to decide. "You may go back to the village and tell the people that we shall do them no harm," he said.

Sung ran back to his neighbors with great gladness in his heart. The village was saved. He had carried out the little teacher's peace assignment. Who knew but that his neighbors would now be more open to the gospel he had tried to bring them?

Little did Catherine Hine know that through her quiet work in London she had prevented an army in China from plundering and murdering a whole village. Through her, Christ had been able to bring the message of peace to many.

No Reason to Be Afraid

Jane Addams   1860-1935

Jane Addams, a strong young woman with a frail, crippled body, cared about people. She cared about them because Christ cared about her. Jane saw the shabby tenement houses in which the many immigrants pouring into Chicago lived. She saw the children running wild in the streets because their parents had to work to make a living. She saw what a hard time the people from foreign countries were having to qualify for good jobs. Their lives were so drab and gray and sorrowful! Jane Addams wanted to share her sunshine and beauty and happiness with these people.

That is how Hull House was born. It was a large, beautiful mansion that was open to all in the neighborhood. Jane had restored the old building and furnished it with lovely things. Nothing was too good for Hull House. But none of it belonged to her. It was for old and young to enjoy. It was their house, and they took pride in it.

Soon there was a day nursery at Hull House for little children. Their happy laughter filled the place. There were interesting activities for older children. There were classes for adults. And always Jane was there to counsel and to help in whatever way she could. When money was given for Hull House, Jane kept nothing for herself. She used it to help as many people as possible.

Since she owned nothing and the house belonged to all, Jane Addams did not need to be afraid that anything would be stolen. And usually nothing was taken. But one night something unusual happened.

Jane was asleep in her bed, and her little nephew who lived with her after his mother died was asleep in the next room.

Suddenly Jane was awakened by a strange noise. A man was rummaging around in her room!

Jane's first thought was that the intruder might wake the little boy, so she said to him in her calm pleasant voice, "Shh, don't make a noise!"

The burglar was so startled that he rushed to the window to climb out and get away before he was caught.

Quietly Jane Addams said to him as she would have said to any of the children who came and went at Hull House, "Don't go down that way. You might hurt yourself. Go out in the hall and walk down the stairway!"

The man obeyed her! Jane heard him hurry down the stairway and out of the door. Then everything was quiet.

Since Jane Addams possessed nothing that her friends could not share, and since she was first of all interested in the welfare of other people, even burglars, she was not afraid. That was her best protection.

A Voice for Peace

Jane Addams   1860-1935

When World War I broke out, Jane Addams was greatly troubled. She had tried to help the people of many different races and nationalities learn to live peacefully side by side in the neighborhood of Hull House. In Hull House, the community center in Chicago of which she was in charge, all were treated alike. For many years, Jane had also worked for international peace. Based on her strong Christian faith, she believed that if individual people could learn to solve their problems without violence, nations should be able to do the same.

Now in wartime, countries that called themselves Christian were shooting at each other. Now even those who said they were followers of Christ hated each other. Now there was misery, there was destruction, and there was death everywhere. And anyone who said that war was wrong was called a traitor.

People who had previously thought that war was horrible and stupid were no longer so sure that war was unnecessary. People who had always said that war solved no problems no longer dared to say it. People who had believed in Christ's love for all people now behaved as if Christ's love belonged only to the people in their own country.

Would Jane Addams also change her views now?

No, she went right on saying, "War is wrong!"

She said it to individual people.

She said it in churches.

She said it from public platforms.

"We are wrong in hating other people. We are just as wrong in killing other people as they are in killing us. We must learn to know and under-stand each other. Then there will be no need for war."

To talk like that was not considered a patriotic thing to do.

Many of Jane's friends would not speak to her anymore.

Newspaper editors said she was not a good American. They called her a traitor.

Some men and women did not come to Hull House anymore. They were afraid to be seen with Jane Addams.

All this hurt Jane very much, but she could not go against her conscience. Instead of helping to kill more people, she worked with the government's Department of Food Administration to keep them alive. She loved her country so much that she wanted to make it a better place in which to live.

When the war finally ended, Jane wanted to make sure that the horror of it should never happen again. Together with women from many other European countries, including former enemy countries, she helped to form an organization called the Women's International League for Peace and Freedom. All the women who belonged to it wanted to work for peace in the world. For fourteen years Jane presided over the meetings of this league and worked very hard to alleviate the suffering that had been caused by war.

Toward the end of Jane's life something very beautiful happened. Her efforts in behalf of peace were internationally recognized. In 1931 she was given the Nobel Peace Prize.

The voice of peace was heard all over the world!

God Heard My Prayer

Enos Stutzman   1918

The First World War had broken out, and Enos Stutzman did not know what to do. All the boys his age were called up to serve in the army. He knew he would have to go, too, but he did not want to.

Enos loved his country.

He loved his parents.

But above all, he loved God. Enos did not want to kill anyone.

When he received his draft notice in July of 1918, neither Enos nor his parents knew how he could convince the government that he was a conscientious objector at heart. All they knew was that you had to obey a call from the government.

There was no one to help Enos.

There was no one to give him advice.

There was no one to stand with him.

All alone at night Enos fought his awful battle. Fortunately, Enos had always talked things over with God. His mother had taught him that from childhood on. So now in his agony, he said to God, "Father, I don't want to kill anyone. I know that you don't want me to do that. Your Son Jesus Christ loved everyone, and I want to follow him. But I have not learned how to say it before people so they will believe me. Please help me. Please lead me in such a way that I won't need to kill anyone."

Enos's father and mother were very much concerned about him. They loved him dearly. It almost broke their hearts that their son had to go into the army. Far into the night they talked together. They could not find a way out. The next morning Enos would have to go to Camp Funston.

Finally Enos said, "Mother and Dad, no matter what happens, I promise you, I will not kill anyone. I am sure God will do a miracle so that I won't have to."

With that conviction Enos went into the army. He put on a uniform. Suddenly he looked the same as the eighty-five thousand other men at the camp. He felt as if they were all little parts of the same huge machine—a machine out to destroy human beings.

Enos knew he did not belong there.

He did not believe in what they were doing.

He was afraid of what was to come.

But every day he obeyed the orders because he did not know what else to do. And every day he prayed to God to help him out of his terrible dilemma.

After about a week in the army, all the men in the company to which Enos belonged were ordered to go to the theater. There, in preparation for combat, they were made to see with their own eyes what war was really like.

They saw the killing.

They saw the slaughter.

They saw the hatred for the enemy in the soldiers' faces as they charged.

Enos was almost sick to his stomach. He was sitting in one of the back seats of the theater, so he walked out. He couldn't stand it any longer. It was the most dreadful, gruesome thing he had ever seen.

"Lord," he moaned, "is this going to be my fate from now on? Deliver me, O my God, deliver me from being part of it."

Every night Enos cried himself to sleep. But he still had the faith that God would help him. "Lord," he said, "you see me. You know I want to get out of this. I do not want to kill. Show me a way so that I won't have to do it."

In the morning he was part of the army again.

"Forward, march! Left, right, left, right!" shouted the commander, and all the seventeen-hundred men of his company marched.

One day as they stood ready, one number was called out. His number! Of all the seventeen-hundred men, his number was called! Numbly Enos stepped out of rank. What was this?

The commander asked him to carry a message, that was all. Soon he was back again and fell into rank as the men marched.

But the following morning, Enos was called out again. This time he was told that he was not to be a part of the daily drill, but that he was to go to Bugler School to learn to play the bugle!

His heart lifted. Buglers did not carry arms. They followed after the battle and took care of the wounded. Was God beginning to answer his prayer? Was the miracle happening?

But how could he play the bugle? He had grown up in a church where all instruments were against the rules, and so he could not read notes. He couldn't see how God would tell anyone how to read notes on the spur of the moment even in a miracle. He had better get busy, otherwise he wouldn't get into the bugle corp.

Enos was not qualified for anything but driving a team of horses at that time. To get into the bugle corp, especially a high-rated organization like the military band, was the last thing he could have dreamed of. Yet, in twelve days Enos memorized fifty-five regimental calls. He got the job! Even the military men could not understand how it happened.

The time came when Enos marched at the head of his company.

He blew his bugle loud and clear.

He **blew** it jubilantly—toot, toot, toot!

God had answered his prayer. God had performed a miracle in his behalf. He would not need to kill anyone!

To Pay or Not to Pay

John Schrag   1918

John Schrag was a man of character. He was a man of conscience. He was a man faithful to Jesus Christ.

John Schrag was the kind of man who would have a very rough time if ever a war should break out and hate and violence become a virtue. And sure enough, it did.

In the tense days of 1917 when the United States entered World War I, everybody in his community in Kansas was supposed to hate the Germans. John Schrag did not hate them. Why should he hate anyone?

Everybody in his community was supposed to buy war bonds to pay for the war. But John Schrag did not buy war bonds. Why should he? He did not want to kill anyone, and he did not want to pay someone else to do so.

This made his neighbors very angry. They tried and tried to persuade John Schrag to buy war bonds. Their patience was running out.

On November 11, 1918, when the war was over, five carloads of men drove out to John Schrag's farm to get him to join in the Armistice Day festival in the town of Burrton. "We'll convert that slacker and make him a patriot!" they said.

When they came to the farm, they ransacked the farmstead and forced their way into the house. They grabbed John Schrag and pushed him into one of the cars. He offered no resistance. He did not even argue with them.

When they came to Burrton, a crowd quickly gathered around John Schrag.

"Buy war bonds or face the consequences!" they yelled.

"No," said John Schrag calmly. "I will not buy war bonds because that is against my conscience. But I will contribute $200 to the Red Cross and the Salvation Army."

The crowd grumbled angrily. They thrust an American flag into his hand. "Salute it," they shouted.

"No," said John Schrag. "My highest loyalty belongs to God."

The flag fell out of his hand. The people were shoving and pushing until suddenly someone shouted, "He stepped on the flag!"

With that the crowd became a howling mob. They cursed John Schrag. They spat into his face. They slapped him. They beat him. They kicked him. He never said a word. He just looked up as if he were praying.

Then a man ran to a hardware store and got a gallon of yellow paint. He pulled the lid off and poured the paint over John Schrag's face. It ran over his eyes, his face, his long beard, and his clothes.

The mob had not had enough. They ran to the hardware store again and got a rope. They put it around John Schrag's neck and marched him to a tree near the city jail to hang him.

At that point, however, the deputy sheriff said, "Now, boys, you've gone far enough. This man is not going to be hung as long as I'm alive." He shoved John Schrag into the jail and shut the door.

In the jail, John Schrag was placed on a raised platform so passers-by could see him through the window in the jail door.

Later John Schrag was released. But one member of the mob who was sorry for what he had done could never forget John Schrag and what happened that night. "Some kind of glow came over his face," he said. "They'd slug him on the one side of the face, and he'd turn his cheeks so they could slug him on the other. He exemplified the life of Christ more than any man I ever saw in my life."

Friendliness Conquers Hostility

Eva von Tiele-Winkler

Eva von Tiele-Winkler was a very well-known and loved deaconess-mother in Germany. She was born and grew up in a castle, but after she had dedicated her whole life to Christ, she gave away her fortune and was a servant to all.

There are many delightful stories about "Mother Eva," but one of the most delightful took place on board a train.

Mother Eva always made it a practice to travel fourth class. One cold, rainy day she boarded a train somewhere in Mecklenburg and found a seat in a compartment. In her hands she carried a bouquet of lovely roses that some of her friends had given her before her departure. The rain drummed against the windows—all was gray and dreary inside.

Soon the door of the compartment was yanked open by a group of people who were desperately looking for a seat. But the occupants of the compartment called out angrily, "There is no room here!" The air was thick with hostility and rejection.

Mother Eva jumped up and with her usual genuine friendliness said, "there is one place vacant here. Just come in!"

She let a little old woman take her seat and then wrapped her own shawl around the shivering woman's thin shoulders.

The little old woman looked gratefully at Mother Eva, but all other people in the compartment were morose and silent. Wet and dejected, they stood or sat in stony isolation from each other.

Then Mother Eva pulled out a rose from her bouquet and gave it to a crying child. Then she gave one to a troubled teenager. It wasn't very long until Mother Eva had given all the roses away. Old and young, men and women, each received a rose. Surprised, they inhaled the fragrant loveliness.

The rain continued to splash against the windows, but inside the compartment it was suddenly warm and comfortable. Strangers were sitting a bit closer together, and Mother Eva, whom someone had now offered a seat, was chatting warmly with those around her.

Friendliness had quietly but surely conquered hostility in a train compartment!

The Christmas Money
1917

When the Czarist government in Russia collapsed in 1917, a reign of terror began. There was no organized government. Bands of outlaws roamed the country, plundering, raping, and killing wherever they went.

These bands usually came at night. Children were well aware of the danger. They were terribly afraid when these men entered their homes.

It was shortly after Christmas. The children in the Mennonite villages had all memorized a *Wunsch* or a special recitation for Christmas. It was the custom at that time that each child recited the Wunsch to parents, grandparents, and other relatives as they visited in the home during the holiday season. Usually children got a *Kopeke* or small coin after each recital, so they collected a number of these coins. They called them their Christmas money.

One night the dogs on the yard of the Klassen family started barking. Everybody was up in a flash. They knew the bandits were coming! They huddled together in a little group. The children clung to their parents' hands.

Soon there came the usual pounding on the door, and the rough shouts demanding entrance.

Father Klassen opened the door. The bandits rushed in, grabbed Father Klassen and his oldest son, and placed them against the wall.

"Give us money," they demanded.

"All our money has already been taken by others who have come before you," said Mr. Klassen.

"Then we will shoot you," stated one of the bandits coldly.

One of the children, a little girl about ten years old, walked over to the bandit and said, "I will get my Christmas money."

She ran out of the room, and before the bandit knew what was happening she was back with her money. She put the little coins into the bandit's hand.

For a moment there was complete silence in the room. Then the bandit bent down and kissed her.

Silently the bandits left the house. There was no shooting that night, and nothing was taken.

As was the custom in that home after these terrifying experiences, they all knelt down as a family, and Father thanked God for his gracious protection. God has many ways his wonders to perform!

Self-Defense

Kornelius Lehn

The Revolution of 1917 in Russia turned the world of the Mennonites upside down. Bands of robbers stomped through the orderly households and grabbed and tore and smashed whatever they could lay their hands on. They took horses and wagons and demanded food and money and service. But, worst of all, there was torture and rape and murder. No one was safe.

Kornelius Lehn was doing some deep thinking. He had grown up in a Mennonite village. All his life he had gone reverently to church on Sundays. His parents and his teachers had taught him to love and honor God. And always it had been assumed that as followers of Christ they were all nonresistant.

But did following Jesus Christ mean that he, a young man, should watch while these ruffians were destroying all he held dear? Should he stand by while they were murdering his family members? Should he just let them kill him without putting up a fight? Kornelius' black eyes flashed. Never! Horror was stalking through the villages. These were extraordinary times, and they must defend themselves.

Other young men thought as he did. They got together on the street corners of the village; they whispered about it behind closed shutters; they started talking about it to their elders.

Finally a village meeting was called. Kornelius jumped up. He spoke up bravely and clearly. "We must protect ourselves!" he said. "If we don't do something soon, we shall all be killed."

Kornelius' father was at the meeting too. He looked sadly at his young son, but said nothing.

"No, no," said the minister. "We must seek God's help and protection. Our only hope is in him."

"God helps those who help themselves," muttered Kornelius' friend. "I don't see God stopping all these atrocities. He must want us to do something about it."

"Hush, young man," said an old man sternly. "Who are you to criticize the Almighty?"

The argument went back and forth. They came to no mutual agreement. Finally a determined minority formed a resistance group called the *Selbstschutz* or "Self-Defense." Kornelius was one of them.

He assured his father, "We are not an army unit, Father. It is not as if we are going out on purpose to kill anyone. All we want is to defend the villages."

But to defend themselves they had to have guns and ammunition.

And to use the ammunition wisely they had to plan strategy.

Often the best strategy was to take the offensive. And to carry on an offensive, they had to shoot.

And so the Mennonite men learned to shoot. But they shot with a heavy heart. And they shot with a bad conscience. They shot because they saw no other way out.

Kornelius tried not to think of his father as he stormed ahead. And he tried not to think of the words of Jesus before his crucifixion, "Put your sword back into its place; for all who take the sword will perish by the sword" (Matt. 26:52, RSV).

The little band of resistant Mennonites fought bravely. Over and over again they saved people in the villages from certain death. Many times they performed feats of unbelievable courage.

But finally they were overpowered by the sheer numbers of the opposing army. And then retribution came.

For a long time, they had been searching for Kornelius, since he was one of the leaders. And finally they found him.

Kornelius walked with them straight and tall. And when they tortured him in order to make him give them the names of other young men in the Selbstschutz, he said, "No, I will not tell you. You have me. That is enough."

Kornelius was killed. Kornelius' father was killed. And so were many members of the Selbstschutz who had so bravely set out to save their villages.

Were the men in the Selbstschutz brave or merely foolish? Were they doing their duty, or did they lack faith in God? What do *you* think they should have done?

Do You Really Believe in God?

Aron P. Toews   1935

88

It was the winter of 1935. In the Mennonite settlement of Chortitza (Ukraine) and in the surrounding area, most of the ministers had already been arrested and banished.

The last of the ministers, Aron P. Toews, was in prison for many months. After an endless number of cruel cross-examinations in which the authorities tried to get him to renounce his faith in God, he was stuck into a small cell with young criminals. Mr. Toews had heard from other prisoners how inhuman these boys could be. They had grown up without parents, had organized themselves into street gangs, and lived through thievery until they were arrested by the police.

The officer who accompanied Mr. Toews unlocked the door of the cell and pushed his prisoner in. Before he locked the door again, he said to the boys, "Here you have a preacher! Do what you want with him!"

In an instant the gang was upon him. "Give us tobacco! Give us something to eat!" they yelled in menacing tones.

For a while Mr. Toews stood quietly at the door. He knew he was completely powerless in the hands of these bullies.

Then he said to them, "Listen carefully. It is true that I am in your power, but remember this: you as well as I are under a higher power. That is God. You cannot do anything that God does not see!"

A howl of rage was the answer. Some grabbed the bundle that Mr. Toews was carrying and tore it to pieces; others jumped on him and pounded him to the floor. They tore the false teeth out of his mouth and took his warm blanket. He had to sleep in his coat on the bare cement floor.

One night when everyone in the cell was asleep and the moon was shining through the little barred window, something stirred. Mr. Toews felt something tugging at his sleeve. When he raised his head he looked directly into the pleading eyes of a young boy.

"Grandfather," whispered the lad, "tell me something about your God. Do you really believe in him?"

Mr. Toews sat up as comfortably as he could and started telling this boy God's story of salvation. Gradually more and more boys awakened. They raised their heads and listened quietly. Aron Toews told them about the love of God which was for each one of them and which surrounds the whole world.

The next morning there was a different atmosphere in the cell. Mr. Toews did not know how much of the conversation had been absorbed by the boys, but he looked into the future with new and vital hope. He was convinced that the love of God has no limits.

Thankful that he had been able to serve God in prison, Mr. Toews later went into banishment. At his side walked the boy who had awakened him that night. This boy had found the Savior!

Children of the Same Father

Around 1930

There was a time in Russia when people were greatly oppressed. Many were sent to the mines to work and experienced great hardship. The cruelty of the officers in charge made life almost unbearable. The foremen ranted and raved and took any opportunity they could to break the spirit of the prisoners.

But one supervisor was different. All the men noticed it. Whenever this supervisor gave an order, he did so in a kind, firm voice. He looked at the prisoners with respect. He did not expect the impossible from them. Whenever he could, he tried to give them some measure of relief in their misery.

One man who had been sent to the mines often wondered about this supervisor. What made him so different from the others? Could he possibly be a Christian? The expression on his face was so peaceful. The prisoner wished he could find out, because he himself was a follower of Christ and felt very lonely not knowing whether there was anyone else there who served the Lord. But how would he ever know? He did not dare to go to the supervisor and ask him, since being a Christian was considered a terrible crime.

One day the prisoner happened to meet the supervisor in a hallway. Quickly he stepped up to the supervisor and said in a low voice, "You are different. Tell me, why is it that you are so kind to us?"

The supervisor looked at the prisoner and then said guardedly, "I have a father who taught me to act in this way."

The prisoner gasped. He said, "Could it be that we have the same Father?"

A light went up in the other's face. The two men looked at each other intently and then clasped hands in a firm handshake. They knew! They knew without a shadow of a doubt that they were both children of their heavenly Father and could trust each other. Acting like a child of God had given the supervisor away.

That is how a church of Jesus Christ was started in that remote area of Russia. Now that they each had someone else for support, the two men gained confidence and gathered other believers around them. The church grew. Even now after most of the exiled men have returned home, there is a fellowship of believers there that is salt and light in a world of darkness.

Communion
The Old Priest   1938

It was the year 1938. In a prison in Russia about two hundred fifty miserable men were herded together in one small cell. Among them was David Braun.

Soon David became especially aware of a Greek Orthodox priest in their midst. The old man had been thrown into prison because of his faith. His peaceful, radiant face made him stand out in that awful place like a candle in the dark. You couldn't miss him.

It was probably because of this that he became the target for the sarcastic and blasphemous remarks of two of the prisoners. They were continually harassing him. They bumped into him. They mistreated him. They mocked everything that was holy to him. But always the priest remained gentle and patient.

One day David received a food parcel from his wife. When people are constantly hungry, receiving a food parcel is something that can't be described—it has to be experienced. David opened the parcel! As he looked up, he saw the old priest looking at his bread with longing eyes.

David broke off a piece and gave it to him. To his amazement the priest took the bread, broke it, and gave it to his two tormentors.

"My friend," said David, "you are hungry. Why did you not eat the bread yourself?"

"Let me be, brother," he answered. "They need it more than I. Soon I will go home to my Lord. Don't be angry with me."

Soon after that he died. But never again in this cell did David hear mockery and blasphemy. The old priest, a true servant of the Lord, had fulfilled his commission.

The Night Revenge Died

This story happened in the year 1941, just before the German army invaded Russia in the Second World War.

John Froese was in charge of all the supplies in the village where he lived. The village was called a *collective*. Everywhere he went he carried a huge bunch of keys with him. He could only hand out potatoes, wheat, cloth, soap, harnesses, and other things upon official request. He had to give an accurate account of everything which belonged to the collective.

Sometimes people wanted him to cheat a little. Jake Rempel, the man in charge of the village, was especially inclined that way. He thought he was entitled to special privileges. But John Froese knew that when Mr. Rempel received illegal supplies he used that fact to blackmail people. Mr. Froese was strictly honest, so Mr. Rempel did not like him.

One day Mr. Rempel demanded that John Froese harness teams of horses for a wagon transport to a nearby city on the Dnieper River.

Mr. Froese handed out the harnesses and made the necessary arrangements. Since he had already worked for three days and three nights without a break, he did not wait until the whole transport was ready before going home to have some breakfast.

Just as he sat down at the table with his wife, a carriage driven by a coachman came up the driveway. In the carriage sat Mr. Rempel. Haughtily he demanded that John Froese step outside.

"You are guilty of sabotage. You have tried to harm the state," said Mr. Rempel. "Get back to the office immediately!"

Without eating, John Froese dragged himself back to the office. Mr. Rempel wrote on a piece of paper, "John Froese is guilty of sabotage and I order him to be court-martialed." Then he handed the paper to John. "Here, take this to Mr. Mueller, the superior of the district!"

Mr. Mueller lived in the next village.

John Froese knew that he could be shot. He begged, "Think of my wife and my three little children."

"What do I care about your wife and children?" scoffed Mr. Rempel. "This is my chance to get even with you!"

John Froese dragged himself wearily along the road leading to the next village. His wife was hoeing in the fields when she saw him go by on the road. She did not know what had happened.

When Mr. Froese got to the district office, Mr. Mueller was not home.

John Froese walked back to his own village in order to do his work.

"Well, have you seen Mr. Mueller?" demanded Mr. Rempel.

"He was not at home."

After a while John Froese got up and walked to the next village again. But Mr. Mueller was still not home.

Three times he walked to the district office without success. Time and time again his wife saw him go by on the road. What could possibly be the matter?

Later in the day, Mr. Mueller came to John Froese's village on business. "There he is," needled Mr. Rempel. "Show him the court-martial order!"

John Froese took the paper to Mr. Mueller. John had no idea what would happen to him. Mr. Mueller, who had been a friend of John's in better years, took the paper and tore it up. "Be more careful next time," he advised.

So the matter was settled, but the stress and strain, in addition to the hard work, was too much for John Froese's already poor health. He became very ill and could no longer do his work.

A few days later the German army marched into the Ukraine.

Mr. Rempel, who had benefited from the Communist government by renouncing his Christian faith and practice, now benefited from the Germans by acting as translator for them.

One day the Germans announced, "Give us the names of people who tortured you before we invaded the Ukraine."

John Froese said to his wife, "Now it is Rempel's turn. This is my chance to get even with him."

"Think of his wife and large family," she said, horrified.

"That's what I told him when he wanted me court-martialed," said John. "But he would not listen."

John and his wife did not sleep a wink that night. They talked and talked. In the morning John Froese no longer needed to take revenge. He did not report Mr. Rempel.

Later Mr. Rempel was deserted by the Germans. The Russians captured him, and he suffered much in a prisoner-of-war camp. His large family, left fatherless, suffered much also. According to news circulated among the refugees, Mr. Rempel repented of the error of his ways before he died.

Mr. and Mrs. Froese were thankful that they had not taken revenge. Their consciences were free.

Do As You Are Told!

Frank Keller

Frank Keller was puzzled. And his friends were puzzled. The United States had just entered World War II, and they knew they would soon have to register for the draft. What should they do?

The position of their church was very clear. All young men were expected to register as conscientious objectors. Frank and his friends knew that. They had attended Sunday school and church services faithfully with their families ever since they could remember. But now they had to make their own decision.

Their country was going to fight a war against evil forces. Why was it wrong to be a part of that? True, it said in the Bible, "Thou shalt not kill," but there were plenty of wars described there as the will of God. Christ had said, "Love your enemies," but was that a reason for letting the enemy overrun your country? And were there not many, many people now involved in the war who were Christians? To defend your homeland seemed so noble and right! And besides, some of the boys who were going as conscientious objectors were doing so only to please their parents. Frank and his friends rebelled at that. They wanted to be honest with themselves and others. Was fighting wrong, as their church taught, or was it right?

They did not feel equipped to make the decisions that faced them. Should they automatically register as conscientious objectors regardless of their present beliefs, or should they enter the military? Endlessly they discussed these questions.

And then the time was upon them. Individually they received their draft notices. Individually they made their decisions. Out of a Sunday school class of ten, seven decided to go into the armed services. Frank was among them. He had earlier decided to follow Christ, but he had not reached the point where he could honestly say that war was something in which he could not participate.

So, early one morning, Frank said good-bye to his parents and went off to the induction center. He came to the desk where he was to be sworn in. A Bible lay before him. The presiding officer barked at him, "Place your hand on the Bible and repeat after me."

Frank placed his hand hesitatingly on the Bible. Had not Jesus said, "But I say to you, Do not swear" (Matt. 5:34)? He had memorized the verse in Sunday school.

The man was rattling off the oath, and Frank had no time to think. He heard himself repeating after the man:

"I do solemnly swear that I will bear true faith and allegiance to the United States of America, and that I will serve them faithfully and honestly against all their enemies whatsoever, and that I will obey the orders of the officers appointed over me, according to the rules and articles for the government of the Navy."

What had he done? Frank shuddered. He had sworn allegiance to his country—not to God. Just who was his Lord and Master?

Numb and hollow inside and trying not to let all this bother him, Frank followed the instructions given him. He was sent to the naval training base in New York to receive his basic training.

There he received a tremendous reception. Frank was a very good athlete, and the navy needed men like that. He was immediately made instructor in the drill hall. Finally Frank was beginning to feel a little better. Things were not so bad after all.

But in the morning he had a rude surprise. After everybody had been awakened by a bell, he heard a voice shouting, "Now hear this! Go to the head (men's room)!"

They all did so.

After a bit, the voice shouted again, "Now hear this! Line up and go to the basement to wash and shave."

They all did so.

Then the voice shouted, "Line up and go to the dining hall!" "Go to the drill hall!" This is the way it went all day long.

At first it was all so new it was exciting, but when it continued day after day, Frank was beginning to feel like a robot—like a nobody. Somebody barked an order, and he automatically responded. He did not have to think. He did not need to make any decisions. In fact, he could not. Someone else made them for him. The awful thought came to Frank that they were all becoming people who would obey any order at all that was shouted at them by a superior. A button could be pressed, a command given, and they would all automatically do it, no matter what it was—no matter how evil it was. They were a huge machine which did not care what individuals thought or felt.

The worst of all was to follow orders during obstacle-course training. They were taught the three vital points in killing a person with a night stick: "Across the nose!" "On the shoulder!" "In the groin!"

Charging ahead at the dummies, the officer shouted, "Hit him! Give it to him! He's a German! He's a Jap! Hit him here! Hit him there!"

The recruits obeyed orders but with no enthusiasm. How could they, with no hate in their hearts?

The officer cursed them all soundly. "He's your enemy!" he yelled. "Hate him, hate him, hate him!"

Frank ran forward automatically, but thundering in his heart he heard the words, "But I say to you, Love your enemies" (Matt. 5:44)!

Oh, God! Oh, God! What had he done? At night Frank buried his head in his pillow and tossed sleeplessly from side to side. He realized now that hatred had to be built up within the hearts of the men before they could kill, and that killing was the business of the military. He had decided to join the military. He was part of it. But he had also decided to follow Christ! How could he do both?

Conflicting loyalties almost tore Frank to pieces, especially when, as instructor, he himself had to teach the recruits the art of killing. What was the answer to his unending questions about conscientious objection and defending his country? Would he ever be at peace again?

In time Frank was sent to a base in Rhode Island. While he was here, the war in Europe ended. At last! Surely now they could go home and somehow all his questions would be answered. He would become whole again.

But the time was not yet. They received the news that they would be shipped to the Philippine Islands. On the way over there, while they were in California, the atomic bomb was dropped on Hiroshima. But this, too, did not end the term of service for Frank.

He and his navy unit went to different islands in the Pacific. Frank thanked God that the war was over and that at least he did not need to kill anyone. But his questions were still there, and his guilt continued to haunt him, especially when he saw how his fellow servicemen treated the native people in the Philippines. *Gooks* they called the Southeast Asian people and treated them like mud under their feet. Even though Frank tried to help the people, he was still a part of the organization that was oppressing them.

Finally Frank's term of service was over and he could go home. Home to his parents, home to his girlfriend who had stood by him in his struggles all these years, and home to his own country. But would he ever get rid of his guilt? Would he ever know what he truly believed?

In the Zion Church in Souderton, Pennsylvania, he found a spiritual home. There a Sunday school teacher whom they called "Poppy" Yoder, and the minister, Ellis Graber, welcomed the returning serviceman with open arms. They and the congregation surrounded him with compassion and understanding. They demonstrated to him that in Christ there is forgiveness. They allowed him to ask his questions and helped him to search for the answers.

After his experiences in the navy he could see many things much more clearly than before.

Feelings which had been vague and unformed gradually became convictions and joyous certainties. He was now ready for one supreme loyalty. He knew he could not serve two masters. He loved his country and wanted to serve it, but first and foremost he now belonged to God.

With an undivided heart Frank Keller set out on an exciting journey—attempting to follow the footsteps of the Prince of Peace.

I Cannot Forgive Him

Corrie ten Boom

After Corrie ten Boom came home to Holland from a concentration camp in Germany in 1945, she started speaking to people everywhere about what she and her sister Betsie had learned through their suffering.

Corrie's sister Betsie, who died in the concentration camp, had been convinced that if people can be taught to hate, they can be taught to love. And if they learn to love, they are more than conquerors. They can forgive.

"We must tell people that there is no pit so deep that he (God) is not deeper still. They will listen to us, Corrie, because we have been here." This is what Betsie had said in the concentration camp.

So at first Corrie bumped through the streets and suburbs of Haarlem on bicycle rims to tell people sick with hatred the good news of God's love. Then after the war was over, she traveled all over Holland, to other parts of Europe, and to the United States. Everywhere she preached the message of forgiveness.

Then one day at a church service in Munich, Germany, she saw him sitting in the audience. It was the former S.S. man who had stood guard at the shower room door in the processing center at the concentration camp Ravensbruck!

He was the first of her jailers that Corrie had seen since that time. And the sight of him suddenly brought back, overwhelmingly, all the painful experiences.

As the church was emptying, the man came up to Corrie beaming and bowing. "How grateful I am for your message, *Fräulein*," he said. "To think that, as you say, he has washed my sins away!"

His hand was thrust out to shake Corrie's. And she, who had preached so often to people who had survived the concentration camp the need to forgive, kept her hand at her side.

Even as the angry, vengeful thoughts boiled through Corrie, she saw the sin of them. Jesus Christ had died for this man; was she going to ask for more? "Lord Jesus," she prayed, "forgive me and help me to forgive him."

Corrie tried to smile. She struggled to raise her hand. She could not. She felt nothing, not the slightest spark of warmth or charity. And so again she breathed a silent prayer. "Jesus, I cannot forgive him. Give me your forgiveness."

As she took his hand the most incredible thing happened. From her shoulder along her arm and through her hand a current seemed to pass from her to him, while into her heart sprang a love for this stranger that almost overwhelmed her.

And so Corrie discovered that it is not on our forgiveness any more than on our goodness that the world's healing hinges, but on his. When he tells us to love our enemies, he gives, along with the command, the love itself.

Taking Christ Seriously

Muriel Lester   1968

Muriel Lester was born in a wealthy home in England. Her heroes were the great generals who with military might had spread the British Empire all over the world. How she loved to read about them! She kept a scrapbook of any story she could find about courage and power during the many wars her country had fought.

But then one day when she was eighteen, she came across the book *The Kingdom of God Is Within You* by Leo Tolstoi. It changed her whole life. It opened her eyes to following Christ in the way of peace. Once her eyes were opened, she could not shut them again, even though it would bring her much heartache and suffering. Tolstoi had made her aware of the importance of doing Jesus Christ the honor of taking him seriously, of thinking out his teaching in terms of daily life, and then acting on it even if ordered by police, prelates, and princes to do the opposite.

Muriel's first problem was to decide how she could take Christ seriously in ordinary, everyday living. She felt that as a peacemaker she must help to purify the world, to save it from poverty and riches, to heal the sick, to comfort the sad, to wake up those who had not yet found God, and to create joy and beauty wherever she went.

In order to carry out this task, she and her sister founded a neighborhood house called Kingsley Hall in a very poor district in London. Here she tried to help people to love and help each other. There were interesting classes for children and grownups; there were opportunities to play; there were Sunday worship services. Muriel Lester brought to these people their birthright of music, art, poetry, drama, camps, open-air life, self-confidence, and the joy of building the kingdom of heaven in their neighborhood.

Because of the extreme poverty of the people,

Muriel Lester decided to become poor herself in order to identify with them. When her father died and left her some money, she let the churches and women in the district use it all to set up a program of home-help for those that needed assistance in times of sickness and stress. Muriel was constantly campaigning against bad housing, rats, slum landlords, and public indifference. She wanted everyone to cooperate with God.

Then World War I broke out. Everybody in England was called upon to help the war effort. Each citizen must give and work and pray that the enemy could be destroyed as soon as possible.

But Muriel Lester spoke out openly against war. She said, "War solves no problems. It is as outmoded as cannibalism, slavery, blood-feuds, and dueling. It is an insult to God and man. It is a daily crucifixion of Christ."

This conviction did not create friends for Muriel Lester. In the midst of war hysteria, people became very angry with her. She received hate letters, people boycotted Kingsley Hall, inflamed patriots threatened her, police came to raid the building, and hooligans harassed her constantly. Finally the center was hit by a German bomb.

But Muriel Lester still said, "At Kingsley Hall we refuse to forget about the Sermon on the Mount until the war is over. We cannot think of God as a nationalist. We cannot suddenly look upon other human beings as enemies just because they happen to have been born on the other side of a river or a strip of sea."

In 1914, right at the beginning of the war, the Fellowship of Reconciliation was formed. Together with other men and women, Muriel

Lester did all she could to oppose war, violence, and falsehood.

When ministers prayed for the soldiers on the front, she asked them, "Don't you believe Christ's command that we should love our enemies?" When they stuttered a surprised "Yes," she said, "Then why don't you at least pray for them also?"

All through the years between the First and Second World wars, Muriel Lester traveled around the world speaking for the Fellowship of Reconciliation. She happened to be in the United States when World War II broke out. Immediately, the war propaganda took hold of people. Her audiences now became very hostile. But Muriel refused to be silenced.

She said, "It seems to me very naive, irrational, and unscientific to believe that we can overcome the evils in the world by killing each other's wives and children. God gave us the Word. It was given publicly, on the first Good Friday, on a hill, in the sight of all. It was the visible demonstration of the only permanent way to overcome evil."

Instead of urging people to give more to build more armaments, she urged the people in America to send food to starving women and children in Europe.

Winston Churchill, who was convinced that a food blockade was necessary to win the war, was very upset. "What is this woman doing, roaming around the world undermining our war policy?" he fumed. "Stop her immediately! Put her in jail!"

Muriel was on her way to South America. In Trinidad Harbor the British authorities took her off an American vessel and kept her under arrest behind barbed-wire fence for six weeks.

She wrote in her diary. "Excess in drink, vice or gambling won't draw attention to you, but thinking independently will. If it leads you to act generously, to identify yourself with the poor or the prisoner or the foreigner or the Negro, the vested interests will be displeased."

Finally Muriel Lester was put in a jail in London. She had been there before—as a lecturer! When she was released, she kept right on serving others.

After the war, Muriel continued traveling for the Fellowship of Reconciliation. She was a witness to the way of life that removes the occasion for armed conflict. She was a peace-maker.

99

Ministry of Reconciliation

A. W. Roberson   1944

100   A. W. Roberson, a black man, moved to Newton, Kansas, in 1944.

He saw immediately that there were many things in this little city that needed changing. First of all, he and his family could hardly find a place to live because no one would sell to blacks. Restaurants would not serve black people. Hotels would not let black people stay overnight. Barbers did not want to cut black people's hair. Everywhere there was segregation and discrimination.

Mr. Roberson saw that this was not right. His father had always stood up for that which was right, and he wanted to do that too. He believed that if he got into trouble because of it, God would take care of him. Did not the Bible say, "Lo, I am with you, even unto the end of the world"? Quietly and gently, A. W. Roberson went about breaking down the walls that separated people in Newton.

He worked with the Chamber of Commerce. He worked with the Ministerial Association. He worked with individual white people. Always his approach was courteous and loving.

One day Mr. Roberson read in the local paper that the Red Cross was sponsoring classes for children in the public swimming pool. He went to the pool and asked, "Does this mean *all* children?"

"I suppose so," said the attendant uneasily, "but I'd better check."

Mr. Roberson was sent from one person to the next. Nobody wanted to say no, but no one could say yes. The pool was segregated.

Finally Mr. Roberson came to the chairman of the Red Cross. After this, a meeting was arranged

with the city council.

"Alright," said the council. "We will agree to admit black children to the pool if you can get the consent of the parents of white children."

That was a difficult job. But God had already provided help.

At the Bethel College Mennonite Church there was a summer Bible school class that planned one hour of swimming every day. The children in this class had many black friends from school and invited them to join them. Olga Martens, the teacher, and some other concerned adults got signatures from the parents of the children that this was alright. And so it happened that the pool manager was presented with twenty-two signatures of parents wanting an integrated pool. That summer black and white children swam together happily.

But this was only the beginning. The ban against blacks was not yet lifted. Mr. Roberson quietly persisted, however, until finally several years later another city council meeting was called. By this time segregation was against the law, so the pool, which had been paid for by all taxpayers, was finally also available to all.

Mr. Roberson stayed in Newton and continued to work steadily at building bridges of friendship and understanding. "I don't believe in violence," he said. "Everything can be realized by peaceful means."

The world may not know about A. W. Roberson. Not everyone in Newton may be aware of him. But God knows that the community has become a better place in which to live because A. W. Roberson made it his home.

I Am Tired

Rosa Parks   1956

Rosa Parks was tired—just plain tired. She had been working all day, and she hoped with all her heart that she would not need to stand in the bus going home. That was all. Little did she dream that the moment was almost upon her when she would be called upon to make a decision so momentous that it could change the face of America.

Right now Rosa Parks just waited for a bus—an ordinary bus in Montgomery, Alabama. The first one that came along was so full that she would need to stand, so she didn't take it. The next one was much emptier. Surely there would be a chance to sit down! Gratefully Rosa sank down in the only vacant seat in the middle section where black people were allowed to sit if no white person needed it. The Negro section in the back was already full. Rosa Parks was still just thinking of getting home and getting her evening work done.

But then at the third stop a number of white people boarded the bus and filled the front section. One man was left standing.

The driver turned around, looked at the four black people sitting in the middle section and said, "I will need those seats."

Because of segregation, this meant that the four black people, including Rosa, would need to stand in the aisle so that the one white man could sit in that section.

At first none of the four people moved. The driver said threateningly, "You all better make it light on yourselves and let me have those seats."

The two women across the aisle and the man beside Rosa stood up and moved out into the aisle.

Rosa just moved over to the window, and sat.

She was suddenly so terribly tired! Not just physically tired. She was tired of all the indignities heaped upon her and her race; she was tired of all the injustices, of all the stupidity. She was tired of cooperating with an evil system that had enslaved her. She had to be free. For the dignity and integrity of her innermost being, the time had come to say no to evil no matter what the consequences.

The driver looked at Rosa. "Are you going to get up?"

"No, I am not," said Rosa.

"If you don't stand up, I'm going to have you arrested."

"Go ahead and have me arrested," said Rosa.

The driver did not ask any questions. He got off the bus and called the police.

When the driver came back he stood in the well of the front door and looked towards the back. He did not say anything. Rosa did not say anything. No one else said anything. It was quiet in the bus. There was no argument and no confrontation.

When the policeman came, he went over to Rosa and said, "Did the driver ask you to stand?"

"Yes, he did," said Rosa.

"Why didn't you stand up?" asked the policeman.

"Because I don't think I should have to," answered Rosa. "Why do you push us around?"

"I don't know, but the law is the law, and you are under arrest."

Rosa got up and followed the policeman. He took her to the city hall to have her booked and then on to the jail.

Numbly Rosa Parks sat in her cell. She was now in prison, but in reality she knew that at last she was free.

Rosa Parks was loved and respected in her community. Word about her arrest spread

quickly. The time was ripe for change. Under the leadership of the young minister Martin Luther King, Jr., a nonviolent bus boycott was organized, and almost a year later, on November 13, 1956, the Supreme Court of the United States declared Alabama's state and local laws requir-

ing segregation on buses unconstitutional.

Quietly and courteously the fifty thousand black people of Montgomery, Alabama, Rosa Parks among them, again boarded the buses. They could now do so with dignity.

I Have a Dream

Martin Luther King, Jr.   1968

104   Martin Luther King, Jr., the black civil rights leader, had a dream.

He had a dream that someday the children of former slaves and the children of former slave owners would be able to sit down together at the table as one family.

He had a dream that someday little children would live in a nation where they would be judged "not by the color of their skins, but by the content of their characters."

He had a dream that someday all of God's children, black and white, Jew and Gentile, Protestant and Catholic, would be able to join hands and sing in the words of the old Negro spiritual, "Free at last, free at last, thank God Almighty, we're free at last."

To make that dream come true, Martin Luther King, Jr., laid his life on the line to end segregation in the United States. He mobilized all the black people to tear down the walls of discrimination. He taught them to do this in love, not hate; with soul force rather than with physical force.

The first attempt at tearing down the walls was to protest the segregated bus system in Montgomery, Alabama. After Rosa Parks was put in jail for not giving up her seat to a white passenger, Martin Luther King organized a bus boycott. He told the black people of Montgomery, "One of the great glories of democracy is the right to protest for right." But he also told them over and over again that if they were hit, they must not strike back. If anyone called them bad names, they must think of Jesus' words, "Love your enemies, bless them that curse you."

So fifty thousand black people refused to ride on the buses until all passengers were treated fairly.

This made many white people who believed in segregation very angry. Someone even bombed Martin Luther King's house. Only by a miracle were his young wife and baby not killed. But even then, Martin Luther King said to his friends who were threatening to retaliate, "Take your weapons and go home. Jesus said, 'Love your enemies.' This is what we must live by. We must meet violence with nonviolence. We must meet hate with love."

Martin Luther King had a dream, and no one could kill it.

Next the people protested the segregated lunch counters. Students and civil rights workers staged nonviolent sit-ins in many, many southern cities to desegregate all public facilities. Volunteers, both black and white, called *Freedom Riders* boarded interstate buses to travel through the southern states and sit in segregated lunch counters.

There were many demonstrations and marches, including a march on Washington. There were many, many legal battles to desegregate the schools. Civil rights workers, both white and black, launched a massive voter registration campaign so that black people could vote.

This made white people who believed in segregation very angry. They insulted the demonstrators, they threw rocks and bottles at them, they beat them, they hauled them off to jail. And many were even killed.

But Martin Luther King had a dream, and that dream would not die.

He personally led many of the marches. Many, many times he too was in jail. He said, "He who accepts evil without protesting against it is really cooperating with it. In order to be true to one's conscience and true to God, a righteous man has no alternative but to refuse to cooperate with an evil system."

Finally Martin Luther King turned his attention to the northern cities. He saw the situation in the urban ghettos. He saw the terrible poverty. He saw the hostility between whites and blacks. It was time to start a nonviolent movement to press for better schools, better jobs, and better housing in the North, too.

Martin Luther King moved his family to a ghetto tenement in Chicago. Then he started an intensive campaign there.

This made white people who believed in segregation very angry. They hurled bricks, they threw bottles. They screamed obscenities.

But Martin Luther King had a dream. And that dream could not be killed.

But the man could be. People had threatened to kill Martin Luther King so often that he knew that probably one day someone would carry out that threat. He was ready to die. "A man who won't die for something is not fit to live," he said.

On April 4, 1968, in Memphis, Tennessee, when Martin Luther King was planning yet another march on behalf of the poor, a shot rang out and killed him. He who had dedicated his whole life to nonviolence died by an assassin's bullet.

Martin Luther King was dead, but his dream was not. That dream lives on in the hearts of many, many people in the whole world. The dream is that some day all people will sit down together at one table as equals. The dream is that some day people will not be judged by the color of their skins, but by the content of their characters. The dream is that some day all God's children will join hands and sing, "Free at last, free at last, thank God Almighty, we're free at last."

A Third Way
The Mau Mau Rebellion 1954

106

The Christians in Kenya found themselves in a terrible dilemma. The black people in the country were rising up against the white government and demanding that the Christians do the same.

"The white people have oppressed us long enough," cried the rebels. "It is time to kill them!"

Banded together in an organization called the *Mau Mau*, the rebels demanded that all Kenyans join their organization and take the Mau Mau oath.

"If you don't join us," they threatened the Christians, "we will know you are traitors who are helping the foreign government, and we shall kill you."

But the Christians had been taught to love, not hate. They had been taught to love their enemies. They had been taught that it was wrong to kill. What should they do? Join the Mau Mau and disobey Christ, or refuse to join the Mau Mau and be killed as traitors? It seemed that there were only those two choices.

Many church members, faced with this terrible decision, joined the Mau Mau, took the oath, and participated in the reign of terror.

Those who decided to obey Jesus refused to take the oath, to carry spears, or to kill. They could not become a part of the Mau Mau resistance. They said, "The only way we can go to the Mau Mau is with the Bible and with love. We love the terrorists and we love the white people. We don't love the sin of the terrorists or the sin of the white people. We love and pray for them all."

These faithful followers of Christ were scattered all over the country, some of them very much alone. One by one they were being killed by the Mau Mau for not joining them.

"We must ask God what to do," said three of the leaders of the church. "Surely God will show us a way."

Every morning they met together to pray. Every morning they met together to think. Every morning they met together to try and find a solution to their terrible problem.

While they were praying, God showed them that there were not only two choices. There was a third one. They decided to turn the school buildings of the Weithaga station into a Christian camp. Now Christians faced with the choice of either joining the Mau Mau or being considered traitors to their country could flee to this camp.

On February 16, 1954, four hundred men and women came to Weithaga. They were choosing a third way—neither for the Mau Mau nor for the government, but for Jesus Christ.

They prayed fervently and the Lord showed them plainly that it was not for them to fight.

They said, "We do not want to fight the Mau Mau. Our work is to pray for them. If we meet them we may be able to help them by giving them the Word of God. If they hate us, we will not hate in return. They are our brothers and we love them. As to the white men who are killing our people, we love them, and whenever we meet them it is our duty to warn them and to give them the Word of God. We love our white brothers for they are children of God also. What does the sinner need? He needs love. Therefore, love is our only weapon."

Someone opened the Bible and read the words, "Not by might, nor by power, but by my spirit, saith the Lord of Hosts." They were content. God had spoken. They would not take up arms.

Many of the Christians who were gathered at the Weithaga Camp were also beaten and bruised and killed by the Mau Mau, but the people there had the security of each other. When one of them was killed, all gathered to celebrate as if it were a wedding day, and they buried the person, praising Jesus.

A few years later the rebellion was over and peace returned to the land. Now many of those who had been fighting, beating, and killing the Christians came out of the bush and repented.

They had seen the strength and joy of the Christians and turned to Christ also and were saved. Twenty years later, many of them were evangelists, pastors, and deacons in the church.

"But if we had had hatred in our hearts and joined with those who were fighting and killing," said the Christians who had gone through the suffering of the Mau Mau rebellion, "there would have been a great separation, and the door would not have been open for them to come back to Jesus and to repentance."

Fallen in Battle

Kornelius Isaak   1958

108

The Mennonites in Paraguay were afraid of the Moro Indians. The Lengua and the Chulupie tribes were friendly. There was constant give and take between them and the Mennonite settlers. But the only time the Mennonites became aware of the Moros was when someone was murdered. The Moros would come stealthily, attack an outlying Mennonite homestead, and then melt away again as gray shadows into the Chaco bush.

And now they had done it again. With terrible shrieks and armed with spears they had suddenly broken out of the primeval forest and attacked the outpost of an oil company not too far away.

"If others are willing to risk their lives even for oil, then surely we should be willing to risk our lives to win the Moros as friends and to tell them that God loves them," said the Mennonite missionaries. For many years they had tried to meet the Moros. Now they were convinced that they must try again.

For this missionary journey it was not necessary to go overseas. Kornelius Isaak, David Hein, and Johann, a Christian Lengua Indian, simply packed a jeep with supplies and drove 200 kilometers to Moro territory. They were allowed to stay at the oil company headquarters.

After making camp, the three men made their first trip to the area where the last Moro raid had taken place. They got out of the jeep. All was quiet. Only the sun danced on the leaves of the trees. Carefully they searched the bush for signs of the Moros. But they found nothing.

The next day they drove out there again. But still all was quiet.

They drove to the place again and again. Had the Moros really left the area, or were they only hiding?

But finally, finally they saw something—

footprints of human beings in the sand; and after a careful search, a sign! Three sticks had been pushed into the ground, with their tips pointing west. On each stick was fastened a feather ornament, and three more sticks were lying on the ground.

What could this mean? They stood around the sign and puzzled over it. But even Johann did not know its meaning.

Finally Kornelius said, "Well, even if we don't understand their sign, we will put up a sign of our own. Perhaps the Moros will understand it."

They stuck a stick into the ground, just in front of the Moro sign, and tied three shirts to it for the Moros to take as gifts.

Anxiously they waited to see whether the Moros would accept their gifts. But the next time they drove out, the shirts were still hanging there. And a camping place showed that the Moros had been there recently, so they must have seen the gifts.

How they prayed that the Moros might understand what they were trying to say and accept their friendship!

One day the shirts were gone! On another day there was a change in the Moro sign. And on still another day there was a framework with Moro feather ornaments fastened to it. Had the Moros left gifts for the missionaries? They did not know. They never saw the Moros themselves.

But one day it was different. Suddenly as they rounded a curve in the road, they saw a group of Moros standing in front of them on the road. Kornelius slammed on the brakes and stopped. The big moment for which they had been hoping and praying had come!

"Boghite dychovay," called David Hein. It meant, "Come here, friend," in the Moro language. Kornelius pulled out some gifts they had brought for the Moros.

With short, quick steps the Moros came running toward them. They took the gifts. But suddenly the car was surrounded by about fifty Moros. Kornelius Isaak felt a stinging pain. A long spear was sticking in his side. Quickly he pulled it out. Then he saw that their Lengua Indian companion was wrenching himself free from the hold of some Moros and reaching for the hunting rifle they carried in their jeep.

"Oh, no no!" thought Kornelius desperately. Forgetting his pain, he grabbed the gun, and he and David Hein set it aside to make the Moros understand that it was not to be used against them—not even after their attack.

"Boghite dychovay," they called again. Then they quickly put out some more gifts for the Indians and drove away.

Because Kornelius had controlled himself so well, David Hein did not realize at the moment how severely he was hurt. But soon Kornelius became unconscious. At the camp he was placed on a plane and taken home to the hospital in the colony of Fernheim.

David Hein immediately returned to the Moros, so as not to lose contact with them again. This time they were friendly and ate and played with him.

Kornelius, however, lay dying in the hospital. In his last hour he prayed for the Moros to whom he had wanted so much to bring the good news of Christ.

After the funeral of Kornelius Isaak, David Hein got up and told the congregation, "The Paraguayan government has now sent soldiers into the Moro territory with strict orders to shoot any Moro they see. Who is ready to go back with me tomorrow before the soldiers arrive? Who will take the place of Kornelius Isaak?"

The next day three young men accompanied David Hein to the Moro people. Kornelius Isaak had not given his life in vain. The wild Moros who had been the enemies of the Mennonites, now became their friends. They were ready to listen to the good news of Jesus Christ who had died for all.

Why Are You Doing This for Me?

A Farmer   1956-1970

In the year 1956 a new area in Alberta was opened up for farming.

The Jake Epps were jubilant. Now they too would be able to get a farm of their own. Jake, his wife, Irene, and their two children, Richard and Betty, made plans. They would need to borrow some money, but they would all work hard. Surely in time they would be able to pay for the farm!

They also looked forward to being a part of a new community. Who would be their neighbors? Would they be able to be friends with them? What would they be like?

They soon found out. When the Epps moved on to their new farm, a man by the name of Ben Strobel had just moved on to the neighboring section of land. When Jake and Ben met for the first time, Jake wanted to shake hands with his new neighbor, but Ben just scowled. "Don't need any neighbors," he snapped, and walked away.

The Epps discussed this incident at the supper table. "We must always be kind to our neighbors, regardless how they treat us," said Jake, looking at Richard and Betty. "This is the rule we live by—the rule taught by the Word of God."

But the intention of the Epps to be good neighbors was sorely put to the test. Mr. Strobel thought of no one but himself. He made life miserable for his wife and for all his neighbors.

The land on which they had settled was open prairie. There were no fences as yet. People had to watch their cattle closely so they would not bother their neighbors. Mr. Strobel, however, let his cattle run free. He did not care how much damage they did.

Mrs. Epp had just planted her first garden. The vegetables had come up nicely when Mr. Strobel's cows clomped all over them. Almost all the tender little plants were destroyed under their hoofs, and Irene was in tears.

The Epps chased the cows off their property but did not say anything.

The same thing happened to the wheat. Over and over again, Mr. Strobel's cattle wandered over the Epp's field and serenely grazed there. Sometimes Jake Epp could hardly contain himself. But what should he do?

One day Mr. Epp and Richard and Betty chased the Strobel cattle off their property again. Mr. Epp drove them right back into Mr. Strobel's yard. Ben Strobel was standing there watching him.

"So, you are bringing me back my cattle," he sneered.

"Yes," said Jake Epp as calmly as he could. "We seem to have a problem here. Your cattle are always wandering over our wheat field and destroying a lot of the wheat. What can we do about it?"

"Well, why don't you build a fence around your land?" growled Ben Strobel.

"Would you be willing to help pay for a fence between us?" asked Jake.

To this Ben replied sarcastically, "You are the one who doesn't want my cattle on your land. Build the fence yourself!"

Jake Epp could hardly believe his ears. He went home depressed. Such behavior was unbelievable!

What could he do? They were deep in debt as it was. How could they afford to build a fence?

Somehow the Epps managed to borrow enough money, however. The whole family worked at digging the holes, pounding in the poles, and stringing the fence around the land.

Finally the job was done. How relieved they were! But to their utter amazement they saw their neighbor, Ben Strobel, striding toward them, purple with rage. He stood in front of them and cursed! "This is a free country," he yelled. "You have no right to keep my cattle from going anywhere they please!"

Jake and Irene and Richard and Betty picked up the tools and silently went home. What could you say to a man like that?

As the years went by, the time did come, however, when the Epps and the other neighbors could say something to the man, Ben Strobel. Ben had been suffering from emphysema for some time. The condition was aggravated by the fact that he was a heavy smoker. One spring he became so ill that he had to go to the hospital. He could not put in his crop!

Jake Epp did a lot of thinking and soul-searching. Finally he went from one neighbor to another to discuss the situation with them. Then one day a whole fleet of drills drove onto Mr. Strobel's land. His neighbors sowed his crop for him!

Mr. Strobel was sick a long time. While he was in the local hospital, Jake Epp faithfully visited him as often as he could.

When he was transferred to a larger town where Betty was now in nurses training, Jake wrote to her, "Visit our old neighbor in your off hours, won't you?" Betty understood. She faithfully went to see Ben Strobel.

When Mr. Strobel was sent to a still larger hospital in the city where Richard was studying, Jake wrote to his son, "Visit our old neighbor, won't you? He needs it." Richard understood. He faithfully visited Ben Strobel.

At last Mr. Strobel recovered sufficiently to return home. But he was far from well. Mr. Epp went to see him.

"Why do you and your family do this for me, when all the time I've treated you like mud?" asked Mr. Strobel one day.

"What do you mean?" asked Jake Epp.

"When I was in the hospital here, you and the neighbors planted my crop. When I was in the hospital in town, your daughter came to visit me. Often she sat and held my hand till two o'clock in the morning. In the city your son came to see me. And now at home you care about me. Why do you do this?"

Jake Epp saw a Bible lying not too far away. He pointed to it and said, "See that Book? What's in there makes all the difference."

Mr. Strobel made no reply, but during the many visits that followed this one, Jake Epp noticed that the Bible was being used. What was in there was making a difference also in Mr. Strobel's life.

We Trust You

Edgar Epp   1969

Edgar Epp knew that there could be violence in a prison when he accepted the position of chief administrative officer (warden) of the Haney Correctional Centre in British Columbia. He also knew that violence on the part of prisoners was usually met with force and the threat of violence by prison staff. Edgar believed, however, that as a follower of Christ he must meet violence with nonviolence; he must overcome hate with trust and love. Would he be able to remain true to his convictions as a prison warden, responsible to the state? He thought the matter over carefully and came to the conclusion that if Christ's command to love our enemies had any validity, it must also work in prison situations. Edgar Epp decided to try it.

One of the first things he did as chief administrator of the correctional center was to instruct his staff to put all the guns in storage. "I do not consider guns necessary in dealing with human beings, including sentenced offenders," he said.

Edgar noted well the uneasiness with which this order was obeyed. After all, if violence should break out, with what could they defend themselves?

The budget included $1,000 annually for ammunition for use in these firearms. It was Edgar's responsibility as warden to order the ammunition, but he did not do so. Why spend all that money for something he did not intend to use?

All went reasonably well for two years, but then Edgar Epp's beliefs were severely put to the test.

It was the afternoon of Easter Monday, 1969. As chief administrative officer, Edgar was off duty. He and his wife and children were driving to a nearby lake to eat a picnic lunch when suddenly the two-way radio began to crackle. Shocked, the family heard these words: "The prisoners are in a riotous mood. They are demanding to meet with the warden!"

Edgar radioed back that he would arrive shortly. He took his anxious wife and children home and hurried to the institution.

Everybody there was very tense. The officer in charge told Edgar what had happened: The prisoners (young adult male offenders, called *trainees* in this institution) were in the playground enclosure. But instead of participating in the normal "holiday" afternoon competitive sports, they huddled in a large group. When the staff tried to break up this unscheduled "meeting," the prisoners responded angrily. They became hostile.

Alarmed, the staff ordered the trainees back into the building, which was located in an adjacent fenced-in area. Some of the trainees went as ordered, but they shouted angrily and pelted the staff with stones they picked up as they passed a gravel pit on the way to the gate separating the two enclosures. One officer was slightly injured. The staff then closed and locked the gate between the two enclosures in an attempt to divide and possibly control the now riotous trainees.

About one hundred thirty of the young men remained in the playground enclosure. This group now broke into the small shed in which were stored gardening and other tools. They armed themselves with such things as rakes, hoes, and spades. Then they set fire to the shed and began milling about, shouting angry insults and yelling, "We want the warden!"

Extra staff had been called to work and at

midafternoon-shift change, all staff were ordered to remain on duty.

After the officer had finished his report, Edgar looked around. To his complete surprise and dismay he saw a number of staff members standing guard with guns in their hands!

"What is this?" Edgar demanded. "I thought I had ordered that all guns should be kept in storage."

"I issued the guns," replied the officer in charge, "because the staff was very much upset that they were unarmed and had no way to control the trainees."

"But there is no ammunition," Edgar replied. "I have not ordered any."

"I know that there is no ammunition," replied the officer. "And all the members of the staff know it, but since the rioting trainees do not know that the guns are unloaded, the staff are bluffing it."

Edgar now knew that the test was upon him. How could he be true to his convictions in this situation?

When the trainees saw Edgar coming, they began shouting even louder and throwing rocks in his direction. They were in a very ugly mood. Edgar felt that his staff members were tense and nervous. They were extremely frightened. They were also very angry at Edgar because they had no ammunition. They wanted strong leadership, but what could they expect when he believed in nonviolence? How could his nonviolent approach spell anything but failure in this potentially explosive situation? Edgar keenly felt the anguish of being all alone. At the same time he had to decide what to do.

Many things raced through his mind. He knew that when people feel threatened, they become frightened and angry. Sometimes they even respond in rage.

"Those trainees are angry because they feel threatened," he thought. "Weapons and angry words will only increase the threat. I must talk to them and listen carefully to find out what it is they are afraid of and then remove the threat."

Edgar began walking toward the fenced enclosure where the trainees were rioting.

"No, no, don't go over there!" exclaimed his staff members. They knew it was very dangerous. Quickly they handed him a loud hailer (bull horn) instead, so he could communicate with the trainees from a safe distance.

Edgar handed it back. "No," he said. "It is unfair if I have a horn to shout them down and they have nothing." He knew the horn was a symbol of power and authority and would in itself be a threat to those who feel oppressed or without power.

As Edgar approached the enclosure, a number of trainees broke from the group and walked toward him from the other side of the fence. Behind him in the institution, trainees were shouting from every window. They wanted violence!

Edgar talked calmly with the spokesmen of the rioters. They told him why they were angry. Some complaints were unfounded, but in some cases they had reason to feel that they were treated unfairly.

Edgar told the spokesmen which complaints he did not agree with. The senior staff members who had accompanied Edgar to the fence nodded in agreement. But when Edgar listed the complaints that were well-founded and explained that he had tried and would try even harder to remove the causes, the staff members were aghast. "Never agree with inmates on anything in a riot," said one officer to him in an aside. "This may encourage them to riot again when they want to make demands."

But Edgar thought differently. "When something is true, I must admit that it is true. Some things they say are true. I must respect the truth and encourage them to be honest. I must let my yes by yes and my no be no."

After some discussion, the spokesmen of the trainees returned to the larger group and reported what Edgar had said. The spokesmen told their fellow trainees that Edgar had promised not to lay criminal charges against them for their unlawful meeting if they would quietly return to the institution, and that he would remove the causes of certain complaints. Edgar had told them, however, which of the complaints were unfounded and had also reprimanded them for being destructive. He had said he would charge the damage to their earning accounts.

The trainees discussed this amongst themselves. "Can the warden be trusted?" they asked. "Will he keep his word?" They agreed that Edgar Epp had given them no reason to distrust him.

The trainees agreed to return to the institution. Edgar instructed the staff to leave their stations around the enclosure and open the gate. The trainees walked quietly to the dining hall. Edgar had instructed the kitchen staff to keep the special Easter Monday meal hot for them even though it was now well past the dinner hour!

Edgar Epp and the Protestant chaplain who had joined him during the negotiations calmly walked into the dining hall also and sat down to eat with the trainees.

The atmosphere was still tense. "Is he crazy?" whispered the staff. "What kind of chances is he taking sitting there in a relatively unprotected area?"

After the meal, a senior officer asked Edgar, "What if they had taken you hostage?"

What if? Edgar had negotiated with the trainees in trust. They indicated that they trusted him. Should he not trust them in return? He only knew that they did not take him hostage or do any other violence to him. And they did not riot again when they wanted to make certain demands. Instead, they asked for a meeting.

The officer in charge that day had seen a new way of responding to violence. He asked Edgar whether he would explain his way of handling a riot at staff training sessions.

Edgar was glad to share what he considered to be good advice from the Master Teacher—love instead of hate! Edgar believes Christ's message is for everyone, including civil servants or anyone having responsibility to the state.

The Broken Fender

Phil Guerena

Phil Guerena was tough. What did he care about these white folks who looked down on him because he was Mexican American? He would show them! Let them be hostile. Let them be abusive. He would do his own thing. Violence was a part of his life in Los Angeles, and he would fight exactly when he felt like fighting.

One night Phil "borrowed" a friend's car without permission. He didn't have a driver's license, but who cared about a little thing like that? Phil was careening down a narrow street, well over the speed limit, when suddenly he hit the side of a parked car. There was a sickening crunch. He knew he had smashed the fender!

Wildly, he wanted to get away, but just then another car came into the street. Phil had to face the man whose parked car he had hit.

Phil saw the man coming out of his house. He braced himself for the usual volley of abuse that he always got when he did something wrong.

"Here it comes," he said to himself, trying to paste the usual flippant grin on his face.

"Son," said the man gently, "are you saved?"

Phil's mouth dropped open. Then, he muttered the first thing that came to his mind. "Uh, uh, I've heard Billy Graham on the radio."

"That's nice," said the man in a warm, friendly voice, "but do you know Christ as your Savior?"

"When is he going to say something about the fender," thought Phil, confused. That religion stuff threw him off. He didn't know how to react.

"Look," continued the man, "come to church with me. We would love to have you."

"Well, I'd better play along with the guy,"

thought Phil. "After all, I have no license, I was speeding, and that smashed fender will come up sooner or later."

Phil went with him. He grinned as he thought, "Wait till the gang hears about my going to church. It'll crack 'em up!"

When Phil came to church he had another surprise coming. The people there were so warm and friendly and funny, and they accepted him so completely as one of their own that Phil almost forgot why he had come.

It was just as he was coming out of the church when he thought again, "When is he going to get around to the fender?"

But the man did not say anything about the fender that night.

He did not say anything about it the next time Phil met him, nor the next, nor the next. In fact he never did mention it at all. Instead, the man kept on being his friend, and Phil kept on coming to that church. The genuine friendliness of the people made the gospel of Jesus Christ that they preached irresistible. Christ took hold of his heart.

Phil Guerena, the tough one, had been overpowered by God's love. He no longer wanted to do his own thing. He no longer wanted to fight. He now wanted to help others find Christ as he had found him.

The people in the church made it possible for Phil to go to Bible school. For many years now he has been a Christian pastor in Mexico, but he has never forgotten the broken fender and the man who never mentioned it.

Turning Sorrow into Christian Purpose

Ki-Byung-Oh and Shin Hyun A. Oh   1958

Ki-Byung-Oh and his wife, Shin Hyun A. Oh, were anxiously waiting for their son to come home. Today he would know whether he was accepted as an exchange student in America.

At last they heard his steps. The next moment In-Ho-Oh came bounding through the door with a big smile on his face.

"God be praised!" exclaimed his mother. "You can go?"

"Yes, yes," cried In-Ho-Oh. "Now it's off to America!"

"This is good news indeed," said his father. "Our prayers have been answered. Now you will be able to study as you wish. And you will be able to study in a Christian country."

"Not only that," said In-Ho-Oh happily. "I'll be in Philadelphia, called the City of Brotherly Love. And they say there will be work for me there so I can pay for my tuition."

The next few weeks were very busy for the Oh family of Pusan, Korea. Mother and father wanted their son to have decent clothing and luggage to go to America. How proud they were of their brilliant son! They used every bit of money they had to buy the things he needed.

And then the time came to say good-bye. It was such a great opportunity for their son, that the parents tried hard not to show their sadness. They would miss him very much. But they knew that In-Ho-Oh would not forget them. Fondly they watched him running lightly up the gangplank of the ship. Their son! Tearfully they waved farewell as he sailed off to America.

Soon In-Ho-Oh's first letter came. He told them all about his life at the University of Pennsylvania. He told them about Philadelphia, the city William Penn founded as a place of religious and racial freedom.

Ki-Byung-Oh and Shin Hyun A. Oh beamed. They were glad that their son was living in such a fine city. They themselves were Christians, and they wanted their son to be under good Christian influence.

In-Ho-Oh's letters came regularly. He knew how anxiously his parents were waiting to hear from him.

But one day in April before the letter was due, the parents received a message that said, "Your son, In-Ho-Oh, was dropping a letter into a mailbox on the street when a group of teenage boys ganged up on him, struck him, and ran away with his wallet. Someone immediately took your son to the hospital, but he died a few minutes later."

In-Ho-Oh's mother and father sat in silence. At first they could not believe this terrible news. Their son, their son! It was too great a shock.

Then they became angry. "I thought he was in a Christian country," said his father.

"And he was living in the City of Brotherly Love," sighed his mother. "How could it happen? How could it happen? Who were those boys that killed our son?"

It took a long time until they could stop thinking about In-Ho-Oh long enough to think about the boys who killed him.

From America came the news that the boys who had done the deed came from very poor broken homes, that they had had no religious training, and that they could not find any jobs. They had roamed around the city in boredom, looking for something to do, and had finally robbed the first person they saw in order to get money to pay for dance tickets.

In-Ho-Oh's parents also heard that the people in Philadelphia were very angry that this thing had happened in their city. They wanted to take revenge. They demanded the death penalty for every one of the teenage boys who had murdered In-Ho-Oh.

Ki-Byung-Oh and Shin Hyun A. Oh shook their heads. "But this is just as hard to believe as that our son was murdered in the City of Brotherly Love," they said. "Did not Christ die for all of us? And did he not tell us to love our enemies and forgive them? No, no, they must not kill those boys."

Quickly they sent a message asking that their son's murderers be given the most lenient treatment consistent with the laws of American government.

Then, after much thought and prayer, In-Ho-Oh's father wrote the following letter to Philadelphia:

"We are not very rich people, by any means. In fact, I could not even send money to my son very often, and he had to work his way through college. I regret now that I was unable to help my son more. So I want to have someone whom I can help now. Our family is gathering a fund to pay for the religious, educational, vocational, and social guidance of these young men when they are released. . . . We want to turn our sorrow into Christian purpose. May God bless you, your people, and particularly the boys who killed our son."

Signed: Ki-Byung-Oh (father)
Shin Hyun A. Oh (mother)

It was only then that Ki-Byung-Oh and Shin Hyun A. Oh could be at peace. Their son's life was over, but they had the faith that far away in America their forgiving love would transform the lives of the eleven boys who had killed him.

117

The Fragrance of a Flower

Que Huong   1975

This is a story about Que Huong (Quay Hoong) and her husband, Ngoc Phuong (Nawp Foong). Names are very important in Vietnam, where they lived, and so it is important to understand that Huong's name means "perfume" and her husband's name means "fragrance." These names would not seem strange to us if we could have met Huong and Phuong, for they were indeed gentle people whose lives were like a lovely fragrance to those around them.

Huong and Phuong, newly married, lived in a little house in Saigon. Huong was a high school teacher in the city. Their life together was happy except for a terrible cloud that hung over them.

Their country was deep in a civil war between the Thieu (Teeyou) government and the Revolutionaries. Brother pointed gun at brother, and everywhere there was hatred and destruction and death. Huong and Phuong were greatly distressed. They longed for peace.

"Come, join the Revolutionary forces," whispered some of their acquaintances. "We will overthrow the cruel, dishonest Thieu government and at last be treated fairly."

"Come, join the Thieu forces," urged other acquaintances. "We must drive the Communist Revolutionaries out if we are ever to know freedom and prosperity."

"We are not Communists and we are not Thieu supporters," said Huong and her husband. "We are for peace. We must end the war."

But *peace* was a very dangerous word to say in Vietnam during the war. You could not even sing about it. Thieu supporters said, "If you are for peace, you must be Communists."

Those who supported the Revolution said, "If you don't fight for us, you must be in favor of the corrupt Thieu government."

Huong and her husband, the two gentle people who dared to dream of peace and who had the truth of God in their hearts, knew that no matter what they did, they would be misunderstood. But they felt they had to do something to save their beautiful country from total destruction. So they participated in a peace demonstration. "Please, please stop fighting," they said. "Let us have peace!"

The Thieu government officials were frightened. "If people are for peace, they will stop fighting for us," they said. "Then we will have no power and money." Quickly they sent the police to arrest the people who were for peace.

Huong and her husband could not return to their little house where they had been so happy. They were both in prison now. There they were beaten and tortured. And finally Huong's husband died. Huong was released from prison to attend his funeral, but was immediately arrested again.

When the war was finally over, Que Huong came out of prison. Since the Thieu government officials had treated her and her husband so cruelly, would Huong now finally hate them and abandon the way of peace?

Someone asked her, "What will you do when you meet the man who tortured you and your husband in prison?"

As Que Huong leaned forward in her chair, it was obvious that she had thought about this many times. She said, "To be honest with you, there will be a little flame of anger inside of me which will want to flare up. But I've got to control it, because if I would kill him, his family would take revenge on me, and then my family would take revenge on them, and it would never end. But the cycle of hatred must stop."

Que Huong and Ngoc Phuong were for peace. There is a saying which is the essence of their story: "A flower will leave a fragrance even on the heel which crushes it!"

It Must Not Happen Again

Keiko Hatta   1970

On August 6, 1945, during the Second World War, the United States dropped the first atomic bomb ever used on Hiroshima, Japan.

Keiko Hatta had just settled down at a desk to start writing. She and nine other girls—all in eighth grade—were required to do some work at army headquarters. These buildings were located in the outskirts of the city, a ten-minute walk from Hiroshima Station.

Keiko did not know that this was the last second of life the way she knew it. The next moment there was a strong, sharp flash. They were all thrown down. Keiko found herself outside the door. After the one blinding flash everything was dust and thick darkness. Keiko could not see her classmates. But after the dust settled a bit, all she saw was horror. The roof of the barrack, in which they had been sitting, had half fallen down. Many of her classmates had been severely wounded by the falling timber. Somebody's blood had splashed on Keiko's breast. "Mother!" "Help me!" Voices, cries, and moans of pain were everywhere. A soldier shouted loudly to the girls to run to a nearby hill for safety. They ran frantically on bare feet.

Many other people in their neighborhood were also running to the hill. Finally they reached a shack on top of the hill and went in there for shelter.

But soon another soldier called, "Can anyone help us?" Keiko and another girl who had not been wounded, immediately went down the hill to help. There were people lying there badly wounded by the crashing houses. Many of Keiko's classmates were still down there. They were dying. Keiko gave them water and tried to comfort them.

Some men, coming from the direction of the city, were trudging toward the hill. Most of them were completely naked and had burnt skin

hanging down from their bodies. Each face was badly swollen. The upper half of their heads, which had been covered with their caps, remained unburned.

In the yard of Hiroshima Station, freight trains loaded with coal caught fire and were blazing high into the sky, lightening the whole hill at night. After a long time, the sun rose.

By six o'clock Keiko started for home, which was situated in another town. She walked west toward Aioi Bridge in the pathless fallen city, not knowing at that time that the bridge was the center of the bombing.

She dodged her way through a mass of black, burned, dead bodies with the smoke around her coming from the still burning remains. As she came nearer to the center of the city, more and more black, burned bodies were lying here and there. She heard something black, which anyone would have thought to be already dead, whispering, "Water, water."

When Keiko reached Tenma Bridge, it was broken down. She was obliged to walk on a railway bridge, looking down the river, where many dead bodies were floating.

Finally she got to Koi Station. Fortunately, a freight train was just about to start, so she got on it. At last the train reached her station, Hatsukaichi.

Her family could not speak when they saw her. It was as if they were seeing a ghost because they had been so afraid that she was killed.

Keiko's life had been spared, but she was sick for a long time. And even after she was better, she experienced many internal diseases because of the radiation from the bomb. The worst of the whole experience, however, was that Keiko could never forget the horrible death of her friends.

Through the years her heart almost burned

with anger when the same questions came over and over again to her mind. "Why should such lovely, innocent young girls be killed? And why were they killed in such a dreadful way?"

Keiko knew nothing of Christianity except that a "Christian" country had dropped the atomic bomb on her city. She did not know that Christ had told his followers to love their enemies and to do good to all people. But for one who had gone through this awful experience, Keiko, after many years of questioning, came to a surprising conclusion. She said, "We can't console the dead souls by keeping anger or hatred in our minds, nor can we bring about world peace by hatred."

It was agony to Keiko to tell of that horrible day. But she did it so that those who do not know of the sufferings of Hiroshima would realize what had happened. "Our future depends on people remembering the past," she said. "It must not happen again."

120

Peace Be With You!

1979

In the year 1979 the governments of the world were building bombs—bombs a thousand times more powerful than the one dropped on Hiroshima. They built more and more and more until they could kill all people on the face of the earth twelve times. And still they kept on building more.

Some people said, "This makes no sense. What is our government doing? God does not want us to kill people. We must find other ways to resolve our differences." So they wrote letters to their representatives in government. They wrote and wrote and wrote letters—thousands of them. And that was good. But the bombs kept right on being built.

Some people said, "God does not want us to kill people. Our government won't listen to us. It will keep on building bombs. We don't want to be responsible for what our representatives in government are doing. We don't want to be part of that wickedness. Let us live simply so we won't have to pay taxes and pay for the bombs." So they lived simply and paid no taxes and did not take part in the evil that was being done. And that was good. But the bombs kept right on being built.

Some people said, "God does not want us to kill people. In a democratic society we are the government. We are responsible for what our representatives do. Perhaps they will listen if we refuse to pay for the bombs." So they refused to pay the taxes that went for the manufacturing of bombs. And that was good. But the bombs kept right on being built.

Some people said, "God does not want us to kill people. But our representatives in government will not listen to letters. They will not listen if we speak to them. They will not listen if we don't pay for the bombs. Let us stop the people from going to the plants where they manufacture the bombs." So they sat on the tracks where the trains ran in and out of the plants. They sat there until they were arrested and taken off the tracks. They allowed themselves to be taken to jail. And that was good. But the bombs kept right on being built.

All the time this was going on, a gentle little woman called Mother Teresa quietly went about her business of healing. Perhaps she wrote letters. Perhaps she spoke to government officials. Perhaps she protested the injustice in this world. But mainly she just went about where the poor and the destitute and the dying lay on the streets of Calcutta. She brought them food and medicine and love. Mostly she brought them love—the love and compassion of Christ which passes all understanding.

And so it was that in the year 1979 Mother Teresa was given the Nobel Prize for Peace. The bombs were still being built, but somehow the world had heard the still small voice of God saying, "Peace be with you!"

Acknowledgements

1. "You Shall Have No Other Gods Before Me" (Pontius Pilate). The basic facts of the incident were taken from *Josephus*, Book XVIII, Chapter 3.

2. "Christ Has Sent Me" (The Apostle John). This story is told briefly in *The Early Christian Attitude to War* by C. John Cadoux (London: Headley Bros. Publishers, Ltd., 1919).

3. "If Your Enemy Is Hungry, Feed Him" (The Legend of Servitor). This story is adapted from a story in *He Had No Revolver* by F. L. Coutts (London: The Bannisdale Press, n.d.).

4. "I Cannot Do Evil" (Maximilianus). This story is mentioned in *The Early Christian Attitude to War* by C. John Cadoux (London: Headley Bros. Publishers, Ltd., 1919).

5. "As the Prophets of Old" (Bishop Ambrose). Adapted from a story told in *Hoeher als alle Vernunft* by Anni Dyck (Basel: Agape-Verlag, 1965), and in *Courage in Both Hands* by Allan A. Hunter (Fellowship of Reconciliation, 21 Audubon Ave., New York 32, N.Y.).

6. "Patrick's Breastplate" (St. Patrick). Adapted from a story in *He Had No Revolver* by F. L. Coutts (London: The Bannisdale Press, n.d.).

7. "What Can One Person Accomplish?" (Telemachus). Adapted from a story in *Courage in Both Hands* by Allan A. Hunter (Fellowship of Reconciliation, 21 Audubon Ave., New York 32, N.Y.).

8. "The Vision of Sir Launfal" is based on "The Vision of Sir Launfal" in *Poetical Works* of James Russell Lowell, 1885, and adapted from a story in *Candles in the Dark*, an anthology of stories to be used in education for peace prepared by Margaret Cooper Brinton, Mary Esther McWhirter, and Janet E. Schroeder. (Sponsored by The Religious Education Committee, Philadelphia Yearly Meeting of the Religious Society of Friends, copyright 1964.)

9. "What Will Happen to Your Soul?" (Baiko San). Adapted from a story in *Courage in Both Hands* by Allan A. Hunter (Fellowship of Reconciliation, 21 Audubon Ave., New York 32, N.Y.).

10. "Ashoka's Edict" (Ashoka, king of the Mauryan Empire). This story is based on information contributed by LaVonne Platt. Her bibliography was: *The Discovery of India* by Jawaharlal Nehru, (ch. 4); *The Ways and Power of Love* by Pitirim A. Sorokin; and *The Outline of History* by H. G. Wells (vol. 1, ch. XXVI).

11. "God Uses the Weak" (Francis of Assisi). This story was developed from information gleaned from various books on Francis of Assisi. The most important of these books was *Blessed Are the Meek* by Zofia Kossak, translated by Rulka Langer (New York: Roy Publishers, 1944).

12. "The Unbaptized Arm" (Ivan the Great of Russia) is based on a story by John M. Drescher in *The Mennonite*, March 13, 1979.

13. "How Did God Conquer Your Heart?" (Mouttet, 1495) is retold from *Tales from Ancient and Recent Mennonite History* by Jacob Janzen, and used in *Through the Year*, Junior Programs (Board of Education and Publication of the General Conference Mennonite Church, 1954).

14. "Free to Love" (Michael Sattler) is based on information in *The Mennonite Encyclopedia*, and in *Mennonites in Europe* by John Horsch (Scottdale: Mennonite Publishing House, 1942).

15. "Never Again" (Christian Mueller) is based on information researched by the late Ernest Mueller, a descendant of Christian Mueller.

16. "Following the Prince of Peace" (Menno

Simons) is based on information in *The Mennonite Encyclopedia* and *The Complete Works of Menno Simons* (Scottdale: Mennonite Publishing House, 1956).

17. "Violence Absorbed" (Elizabeth Dirks) is based on information taken from *The Mennonite Encyclopedia*.

18. "Blessed Are the Merciful" (Menno Simons). This story is based on information from *The Mennonite Encyclopedia* and *Mennonites in Europe* by John Horsch (Scottdale: Mennonite Pulbishing House, 1942).

19. "A Stain and Burden on Our Conscience" is based on information taken from *Mennonites in Europe* by John Horsch (Scottdale: Mennonite Publishing House, 1942).

20. "The White Feather" is adapted from "Die Weisse Feder" in *Hoeher als alle Vernuft* by Anni Dyck (Basel: Agape-Verlag, 1965).

21. "The Cheyenne Way of Peace" is based on information in *The Cheyenne Way of Peace* unpublished curriculum of the Cheyenne Peace Project.

22. "Mr. No-Worry" (Herr Ohnesorge). This story is adapted from an incident in *Lichte Spuren* by Dora Rappard (Basel: Brunnen-Verlag, 1961), pages 113-15.

23. "A Bold New Plan" (Richard Rush and Sir Charles Bagot). Adapted from "A Bold New Plan" in *Candles in the Dark*, an anthology of stories to be used in education for peace prepared by Margaret Cooper Brinton, Mary Esther McWhirter, and Janet E. Schroeder (Religious Education Committee, Philadelphia Yearly Meeting of the Religious Society of Friends, 1964).

24. "What Would Christ Have Done?" is based on information taken from *The Great Trek of the Russian Mennonites to Central Asia* by Fred Richard Belk (Scottdale: Herald Press, 1976). Used by permission.

25. "Why Are You Praying for Me?" (Elizabeth Fry). Adapted from "Elizabeth and the Boot" in *Candles in the Dark*, an anthology of stories to be used in education for peace prepared by Margaret Cooper Brinton, Mary Esther McWhirter, and Janet E. Schroeder (Religious Education Committee, Philadelphia Yearly Meeting of the Religious Society of Friends, 1964).

26. "Father, Forgive Them" (Seth Loflin). This story is adapted from a story in *He Had No Revolver* by F. L. Coutts (London: The Bannisdale Press, n.d.).

27. "I Want Revenge!" Adapted from "Staerker als Hass" in *Hoeher als alle Vernunft* by Anni Dyck (Basel: Agape-Verlag, 1965). Her source was Sammlung de Lange: Lillian Cox, "God's Mighty Men."

28. "Serves Him Right!" (E. G. Kaufman). This story is based on information taken from an interview with the late E. G. Kaufman. The Schowalter Oral History Project, Bethel College, North Newton, Kansas.

29. "Wise As Solomon." This story was told by "Peter Janzen" himself and used with his permission. The name is fictitious.

30. "Could He Ever Be the Same Again?" (Elizabeth Caraman). Adapted from the story "Could He Ever Be the Same Again?" in *Courage in Both Hands* by Allan A. Hunter (Fellowship of Reconciliation, 21 Audubon Ave., New York 32, N.Y.).

31. "In a Prison" (Mathilda Wrede). This story is adapted from an incident in *Ein Horchendes Leben* by Dr. Kaethe Kaiser (Basel: Heinrich Majer Verlag, 1943).

32. "Won't You Have Lunch with Me?" (Mathilda Wrede). This story is adapted from "Red and White" in *He Had No Revolver* by F. L. Coutts (London: The Bannisdale Press, n.d.).

33. "The Little Teacher" (Catherine Hine). Adapted from the story "Die Fahne der Heilsarmeesoldatin" in *Hoeher als alle Vernunft* by Anni Dyck (Basel: Agape-Verlag, 1965).

34. "No Reason to Be Afraid" (Jane Addams). This story is adapted from "Jane Addams' Burglars" in *The Friendly Story Caravan*, compiled and edited by Anna Pettit Broomell (Philadelphia: J. B. Lippincott Co., 1935, 1948, 1949), and from information in other books about Jane Addams.

35. "A Voice for Peace" (Jane Addams). This story is based on information taken from various books on Jane Addams, especially from *Jane Addams, World Neighbor* by Miriam Gilbert (Nashville: Abingdon Press, 1960).

36. "God Heard My Prayer" (Enos Stutzman). This story is based on information taken from an interview with Enos Stutzman. The Schowalter Oral History Project, Bethel College, North Newton, Kansas.

37. "To Pay or Not to Pay" is based on "Gordon" in *Mennonite Life*, September 1975, and "John Schrag Espionage Case" by James C. Juhnke, *Mennonite Life*, July 1967.

38. "Friendliness Conquers Hostility" (Eva von Tiele-Winkler). This story is based on an incident described in *Mutter Eva* by Walter Thieme (Kassel: J. G. Oncken Verlag, 1955), page 220.

39. "The Christmas Money" is adapted from "The Christmas Money" in *Story Collection*, The Foundation Series, copyright 1978 by Evangel Press, Nappanee, IN 46550; Faith and Life Press, Newton, KS 67114; Mennonite Publishing House, Scottdale, PA 15683. Used by permission. The name *Klassen* is fictitious.

40. "Self-Defense" is based on information from Gerhard Lehn, brother of Kornelius.

41. "Children of the Same Father" is based on information given by Helmut Harder after his return from Russia (1979) where Walter Sawatzky told him the story.

42. "Do You Really Believe in God?" is a translation of a story told by Mrs. Olga Rempel in *Einer von Vielen* (Winnipeg: CMBC Publications, 1979). Used by permission.

43. "Communion" is retold from "The Old Priest" by Katherine Janzen in *Story Collection*, The Foundation Series, copyright 1978 by Evangel Press, Nappanee, IN 46550; Faith and Life Press, Newton, KS 67114; Mennonite Publishing House, Scottdale, PA 15683. Used by permission.

44. "The Night Revenge Died" is adapted for telling from "The Night Revenge Died" in *On the Line*, May 1979. All names are fictitious.

45. "Do As You Are Told" (Frank Keller) is based on personal interviews and used with Frank Keller's permission.

46. "I Cannot Forgive Him" is told in *The Hiding Place* by Corrie ten Boom with John and Elizabeth Sherrill (Lincoln, Va.: Chosen Books, 1971), page 215. Used by permission. In the last six paragraphs I have followed Miss ten Boom's wording almost exactly.

47. "Taking Christ Seriously" (Muriel Lester). This story is based on information taken from "No Moratorium on the Sermon on the Mount," an article by Richard L. Deats in *Fellowship*, July-August 1975, pages 15-16.

48. "Ministry of Reconciliation" (A. W. Rob-erson) is based on an article entitled, "Mr. A. W. Roberson - A Peacemaker" by Robert Kreider and used by permission of Mr. Roberson and Robert Kreider. Some information was also supplied by Olga Martens.

49. "I Am Tired" (Rosa Parks) is based on "An Interview with Rosa Parks" in *Martin Luther King, Jr.*, a documentary edited by Flip Schulke, copyright 1976 by The Martin Luther King Foundation, Inc.

50. "I Have a Dream" (Martin Luther King, Jr.) is based on information in many books about Martin Luther King, especially in *Martin Luther King, Jr.*, a documentary edited by Flip Schulke. Copyright 1976 by The Martin Luther King Foundation, Inc.

51. "A Third Way" is adapted from "The Third Way" by Dorothy Smoker in *Story Collection*, The Foundation Series, copyright 1978 by Evangel Press, Nappanee, IN 46550; Faith and Life Press, Newton, KS 67114; Mennonite Publishing House, Scottdale, PA 15683. Used by permission.

52. "Fallen in Battle" is based on "Kornelius Isaak," first written by the author for *Mennonite Churches in Latin America* (Newton, Kans.: Faith and Life Press; Scottdale, Pa.: Mennonite Publishing House, 1971), and on information from "Gefallen im Streit," *Hoeher als alle Vernunft*, by Anni Dyck (Basel: Agape-Verlag, 1965).

53. "Why Are You Doing This for Me?" is based on a true incident related by a pastor about his parishioner. The names are all fictitious as requested.

54. "We Trust You" is based on information provided by Edgar Epp and used with his permission.

55. "The Broken Fender" (Phil Guerena) is based on information from Malcolm Wenger and used with the permission of Phil Guerena.

56. "Turning Sorrow into Christian Purpose" (Ki-Byung-Oh and Shin Hyun A. Oh). Adapted from "My Son! My Son!" in *Candles in the Dark*, an anthology of stories to be used in education for peace. Prepared by Margaret Cooper Brinton, Mary Esther McWhirter, and Janet E. Schroeder. (Sponsor by the Religious Education Committee, Philadelphia Yearly Meeting of the Religious Society of Friends, 1964.)

57. "The Fragrance of a Flower" (Que Huong)

is based on information from James Klassen and used with his permission.

58. "It Must Not Happen Again" (Keiko Hatta) is based on information from *From Summer Cloud*, A Bomb Experience of a Girl's School in Hiroshima. (Tokyo: San-Yu-Sha.)

59. "Peace Be With You" is based on national and international news.

126